In the Heart of Pennsylvania

*T*his book is dedicated to two gentle and
quite wonderful women who were experts with the
needle: my grandmother, Martha Selma Johnson Mehrer
of Lynbrook, New York and Tama Thompson who was
born in Pleasant Grove, Union County and who quilted
most of her life in Loganton, Clinton County.

*Preceding page: Tama Boob
Thompson's crib quilt b. 1891 Pleasant
Grove, Union County d. 1984
Loganton, Clinton County. / Pieced and
appliquéd solid colored and calico
fabrics on white top with plain top.
Applied calico binding. 38¹/₂"×39¹/₄"
with 10-12 stitches per inch. / Private
collection.*

*The filling in this piece is cotton batting
which was the prevalent one used in
most area quilts. It is full of cotton
seeds as were many of the late 19th
century quilts we saw, contradicting the
frequently repeated premise that cotton
seeds disappeared from batting a
decade or so after the invention of the
cotton gin in 1794. Since several grades
of cotton batting were available to area
homemakers that, more than anything
else, might account for the presence of
seeds in the batting. In this case the
seeds are abundant. The crib quilt was
made for Tama by her mother or one of
her grandmothers just prior to her birth
in Pleasant Grove, Union County. It is
in good condition but frequently
washed as nearly all the area crib
quilts were.*

In the Heart of Pennsylvania

19th & 20th CENTURY QUILTMAKING TRADITIONS

JEANNETTE LASANSKY

AN ORAL TRADITIONS PROJECT

Published by the Oral Traditions Project of the
Union County Historical Society, County
Courthouse, Lewisburg, Pennsylvania 17837.

This project is supported by a grant from the
National Endowment for the Arts.

Production and finances: Jeannette Lasansky
Design: C. Timm
Photography: Terry Wild
Typography: Batsch Company, Inc.
Halftones of quiltmakers: Paulhamus Litho, Inc.
Printing: Dai Nippon Printing Company,
Tokyo, Japan.

Library of Congress Cataloging in Publication Data
Lasansky, Jeannette
In the Heart of Pennsylvania
Bibliography: p
Includes index
1. Quilting—Pennsylvania—History—19th
century.
2. Quilting—Pennsylvania—History—20th
century.
I. Title.
TT835.L36 1985   746.9'7'09748   84-29585
ISBN 0-917127-00-5

Cover and inside cover: Stahl family quilt top
Buffalo Township, Union County. Pieced wools
with various colors and stitches in embroidery
floss, dated "1906." 74″×73″. Private collection.

The cover was made possible by donations from:
Business and Professional Women's Club of
Lewisburg, Country Cupboard, Inc., G.F.W.C.
Laurelton Women's Club, Heart of the Country
Gift Shop and Party Plan, Lewisburg Council on
the Arts, Stephen J. Lindenmuth, R.A., Mary
Koons Shop, Packwood House Museum, Slifer
House Museum, Susquehanna Valley Branch of the
American Association for University Women, and
The Union County Historical Society.

Acknowledgments

Grants from the Pennsylvania Council on the
Arts and the National Endowment for the Arts
enabled this project to study and exhibit quiltmaking traditions from Union's contiguous
counties: Snyder, Northumberland, Lycoming,
Clinton, Centre, and Mifflin. Quilts coming out of
strong Pennsylvania-German farm communities,
Scots-Irish homesteads, Welsh enclaves, and the
ethnically diverse coal region, have been
documented. More will continue to be seen
after this study has been published and the
accompanying exhibit is seen at Bucknell. The
slides of these quilts have become part of the
public study collection of the Union County
Historical Society's Oral Traditions Project.

Shirley Bingaman, Betsy Carpenter, Nada Gray,
Julie Kintner, Mary Koons, Diana Lasansky, Joan
Maurer, Martha Root, Alicia Spinner, Elsbeth
Steffensen, Sue Taylor, and Judy Wagner worked
at documenting area quilts and comforts at one or
more of our thirteen sessions held in the seven
counties. The host site or groups that helped
sponsor the documentation sessions include the
Aaronsburg Historical Association, the Centre
County Library and Historical Museum in
Bellefonte, the Clinton County Historical Society
in Lock Haven, the Evangelical Lutheran Church
in Middleburg, the Evangelical Lutheran Church in
New Columbia, the Kauffman Library in Sunbury,
the Laurelton Women's Club, the Mifflin County
Historical Society in Lewistown, the New Berlin
Heritage Association, the St. John's United Church
of Christ in Mifflinburg, and the Trinity Lutheran
Church in Shamokin.

Doris Garthwaite, Bess Huber, and Marjorie
Rosser were organizers of area quilt shows in
Watsontown, Danville, and Williamsport
respectively. They helped me trace owners of
quilts about which I was interested in learning
more. Joan Maurer and Mary Koons, and Gary
Slear especially, expended great effort in getting
others to bring their quilts.

Shirley Bingaman, from Laurelton, an area
resident who has studied quilts all her life, was
important in clarifying pattern names while
Patricia Herr, from Lancaster, served as textile
consultant. Others like Neville Thompson, the
head librarian at Winterthur Museum, were
particularly helpful in keeping me abreast of new
books or projects in this field. I would like to
thank these people in particular for helping me
feel more comfortable with the technical aspects
of the subject.

Also, the Oral Traditions board of directors
provided support and counsel: Richard Steffensen,
treasurer, and George Folkers, Ann Heath, Nancy
Ruhl, Edgar Schnure, and Gary Slear. Julie Kintner,
Rita Moser and Linda Snyder were typists, Elsbeth
Steffensen and Joseph G. Foster were copy
editors, while Terry Wild was the photographer
and Connie Timm, the designer.

My thanks go to all of you, to all whose quilts
were photographed, to all who shared their quilts
and experiences over the past twelve years. It has
been a pleasure.

Jeannette Lasansky
Lewisburg, Pennsylvania
May 1985

Foreword

*N*early twelve years ago, when the Oral Traditions Project was started as part of the county's observance of the Bicentennial, one of the first apparent subject areas was the quiltmaking traditions of the region. Early informants such as Hilda Jeffries from Carroll and Tama Thompson from Loganton had quilts to share—from the most utilitarian and simple, to the elaborate and "just-for-show." The quilts had stories attached to them: stories of owners, of makers, of olden times, and different attitudes. The men and women who possessed these textiles, like *griots,* became part of a generational process of transmitting important cultural information to those who cared to listen as well as to look and touch.

The Project began to photograph area quilts in my home and in the homes of the quiltmakers. On such "quilt days," it was almost certain that not everyone would come at the appointed time, but rather, earlier by a half-hour or more. Puzzled at first, we quickly learned that the reason for the early arrivals and late departures was the desire to share quilts with others who also owned quilts, and to compare. This process went on for several years.

Recently a number of factors converged to make our effort change from haphazard to more studied and intense. It had become apparent that, because of the immense popularity of quilts and their tremendous increase in value, they were coming out of homesteads and leaving the area at an ever-accelerating rate. Also, it appeared that some of the younger quilters were making pieces without the benefit of fully understanding the area's past quiltmaking traditions. They were spurred on by what was considered saleable and therefore desirable in the marketplace, in both old and new examples, and distortion and compromise sometimes took hold. A few of the area's typical color combinations and patterns were discarded while others were simply forgotten.

Preceding page: quilts by Harriet Hull Pensyl b. 1838 d. 1898 Elysburg, Northumberland County. / Pieced and appliquéd solid colored and calico fabrics with some padded work on white tops with plain backs. Applied solid colored binding; front turned to back as edge treatment. (right) 86"×87" and (left) 79" square with 7-9 and 7-8 stitches per inch. / Collection of John and Melodie Persing; Amos and Corine Persing.

Harriet Hull married William Pensyl, a tanner, in 1858 and lived the rest of her life in the old stone Pensyl homestead in Elysburg. Her quilts were probably made prior to her marriage and did not see much, if any, wear. They, along with her coverlet and linens, were stored in this blanket chest which was rediscovered by her descendants when the contents of the house were broken up nearly a century after her death. Padded work, as done on both quilts, is rarely seen in this area of Pennsylvania. The grape motif itself was found only three times in the quilting patterns of other early- to mid-nineteenth century area-pieces and only this one time as an appliqué pattern. The other pieced pattern, sometimes known as Wandering Foot, *was rarely done here also.*

We have found that the passage of the past decade has taken its toll. Women like Hilda and Tama as well as Cora Boop of Laurelton, Millie Leiby of New Berlin, and Bessie Bates Hoffman of Lewisburg, whose recollections had transported us back to the third quarter of the nineteenth century, are no longer alive. Today's "old-time" quiltmakers now talk about the twenties and thirties.

In an effort to understand the area's full range of quiltmaking traditions, it was decided to hold a series of community quilt documentation days, starting first in Union County. Five sites were chosen, scattered throughout the county. Each documentation day was co-sponsored by a local group in an effort to quickly spread the word about the project and to gain people's confidence, thereby seeing the greatest number of pieces possible. After three sessions, held both at night and during the day, it was felt that in each community only a fraction of the extant quilts were being brought in for the research team to examine. Prizes were offered at the remaining days in an effort to bring forth a greater variety of quilts and not just those that families felt were their best. Cash awards were offered for the family bringing in the greatest number, for the piece judged most typical of those seen, for the most interesting and/or complete documentation of a quilt, and for the most unusual item. If there was difficulty in narrowing down to four winners, gift certificates for the forthcoming publication were awarded as well. The award categories were carefully chosen to reflect the emphasis of the project, which was to see great numbers of typical as well as unusual quilts and to get the families to gather the ownership history of their pieces and the story of the maker. We were careful to avoid a category of "the best" since we had already discovered that people tended to leave more ordinary examples at home and we did not want to reinforce that tendency. Radio and newspaper coverage stressed the fact that tops, sample patches, pattern templates, and photographs of the makers were also being sought in this research effort.

The first documentation day following this renewed effort was held in Mifflinburg. Nearly two hundred quilts were brought in by dozens of area families in six hours that afternoon and evening. People were there a half-hour early, waiting for the research team to unpack cameras, film, and measuring tapes. The seven of us never caught up with the crowd until suppertime. It was very exhilarating.

Subsequent days in Union County and then in Northumberland and Snyder counties did not see this trend continue however, so again frustration set in as to how many quilts were still not being recorded. Area quilt shows, held as fundraisers, exhibited both old and new quilts and often had old pieces coming out of homes in areas where a documentation had already been held. These quilts, when added to the numbers seen in the documentation sessions, did however add up to a significant number of pieces, nearly eight hundred.

The project finally hit its stride with the first in a series of afternoon sessions held in conjunction with area historical societies in Lycoming, Clinton, Centre, and Mifflin counties. At the suggestion of the staff at Williamsport's Lycoming County Historical Museum, a Sunday afternoon research session was planned. In an effort to make it an informative outing for families, a half-hour slide/tape show on area quilts, which we had assembled seven years earlier, was projected. The societies' newsletters augmented the usual media coverage.

We were once more inundated with people and their quilts that Sunday afternoon as well as in the other counties we visited subsequently in the fall of 1984. A few people left because we could not get to them soon enough. Some of these quilts were brought to other sessions. People came from counties we had already visited as well as from great distances within a county. Place names like Tamarack, Boiling Springs, Port Matilda, and Lamar; family names like Bastian, Dickey, Gummo, and Kackenmeister; quilt patterns like *Union Square, Basket of Scraps, Ocean Waves* and the *Cockscomb,* were placed before us on the tables. Nearly two thousand pieced, appliquéd and embroidered quilts, and comforts, tops and patches were brought out of boxes, trunks, and blanket chests, and taken off beds—to be shared.

We are convinced that we could do this project again, in the very same areas, and see that same number of quilts or more. In spite of our success in the end, the study of nineteenth and early twentieth-century quiltmaking in the heart of Pennsylvania has just begun.

Union and the six contiguous counties were a good place to start in developing an understanding of Pennsylvania's quiltmaking traditions since its material culture has been overlooked in the past and since its population is an interesting mix of German, Scots-Irish, Welsh, and English; later of Italians, Poles, and Slavs. They were a rural people with few large population centers, many villages and crossroads communities connected to the rest of the state by the Susquehanna River, a system of canals, railroads, and later by turnpikes and highways, yet separated by mountain ridges running diagonally through the region. Their roots were in farming and traditional craft occupations but they were not untouched by sophisticated trends in the more populated regions of the State nor the tastes advocated by national periodicals starting in the mid-nineteenth century. Central Pennsylvania's quilt traditions as put forth in this essay and illustrated in the portfolio that follows, reflect the response of area women to a myriad of cultural factors.

The quilts seen in this research effort came out of family homes primarily or, having recently been taken away, were brought back here for us to see. Some were from the collections of local museums and historical societies, donated by families who sometimes had no descendants. Relatively few were from private collections and dealers. The people involved were acting as caretakers of a great tradition, of a living tradition. They were acutely aware of and sometimes overwhelmed by this responsibility. More than in any other craft tradition that the Oral Traditions Project has studied, this is true of quilts. The hours spent by the quiltmaker in selecting and cutting material (most often scraps from making clothes), in arranging colored fabric and piecing the top, and finally in the quilting, elevate each of these objects, even the most mundane, in the eyes of the owner above inherited or collected baskets or pottery for example.

For this reason, quiltmakers were interviewed at length about their skills and attitudes, and the basic questionnaire that was used follows the portfolio of quilts. Some of the questions attempt to get past myths, whether it be the number of quilts needed for a hope chest or the role of the quilting bee versus that of the solitary individual quilter. The questionnaire should be considered as a starting point for an oral traditions interview. Logical thought sequences have been clustered, where possible, but at times they might not be logical to a particular woman's body of information and also too detailed for some people's quilting experience. The questionnaire has been refined over the course of our project and has proven to be quite useful.

We have deliberately avoided including the quiltmaking traditions of the plain people in Mifflin County who were settled in Big Valley during the time period covered by this project. The background and cultural forces evident in their work are beyond the scope of this study but should be part of yet another.

Where possible, period prose, poetry, advice, instructions, and inventories have been juxtaposed with appropriate quilts in an attempt to understand more fully the cultural setting in which such pieces were constructed. The photograph of the maker is also shown when available and some brief biographical information given. Other caption material attempts to place the selected quilts within the context of those seen in this research effort and to give some statistical information about size, stitches per inch and fabric. Quilt names, when they are indicated, are those arrived at with the family. Though of contemporary interest to owners and historians, names appear to have been of less importance to the original maker. We heard the same remark as did quilt historian Dorothy Cozart of Oklahoma when she was interviewing an old quiltmaker and was pressing her for the pattern's name, "We don't name them. We just made them."

Similar regional and state quilt documentation projects have been or are being conducted in states such as Kentucky, Tennessee, Texas, South Carolina, California, North Carolina, Michigan, and Georgia to name a few. There is an apparent need to strive for uniformity of question concerns and nomenclature, to make the information computer compatible so that local research efforts, no matter how large or small, can become part of a larger body of information on women and their quilts. The Kentucky Heritage Quilt Society has taken the lead in raising the issues involved in such efforts and the American Quilt Study Group is interested in becoming the major repository of quilt research materials. The study of nineteenth and twentieth-century quiltmaking traditions is a particularly exciting and burgeoning one, and we are pleased to be part of that activity since, just like the quilter, we'd rather do our thing than "dust," "mow lawns," "pick stones," or even "eat."

*Quilt by Sarah Wilson b. 1788 New
Hanover Township, Montgomery County
d. 1872 New Berlin, Union County. /
Pieced chintz and calicos with plain back,
dated "1836." Applied white binding.
104¹/₂"×101¹/₂" with 8 stitches per inch. /
Collection of Mary Wilson Boyer Laign.*

*The earliest signed and dated quit is also
the largest. Its large scale rickrack border
formed by triangles sewn together back to
back and off center. Like three of the four
other quilts that date from this period, it is
a pieced star pattern. Forty-seven* Variable
Stars, *forty* Lone *or* Bethlehem Stars,
twenty-six LeMoyne Stars *like this one, as
well as twenty-three* Prairie Stars, *fourteen*
Union Squares *and ten* Feathered Stars
*were among those star patterns done
throughout the time period studied,
1830-1940.*

*W*hen Sarah Wilson and her friend Mrs. Morrison put their final stitches in Sarah's *LeMoyne Star,* they could be proud of a large job well done. The quilt measured nearly one hundred and five inches square. Eighty-one pieced stars made from dress scraps; six hundred and forty-eight diamonds of brown hues formed the stars which stood out on a field of white bounded by a deep chintz border. The women's stitches followed pieced seams, repeated the large triangular shapes seen in the border and set out princess feathers on the white expanse. In the lower right-hand corner, Sarah stitched her initials and the date—1836.

The place was New Berlin, the prosperous seat of Union County situated fairly square in the heart of Pennsylvania. Sarah Wilson's quilt and others by her hand that still exist today—a *Mariner's Compass* and a galaxy of small *Bethlehem or Prairie Stars* interspersed amongst even smaller eight-pointed ones—were part of a shared tradition. Families of English and Scots-Irish descent lived here next to others called Pennsylvania German. By the time that this young woman made her quilt, one of the earliest documented examples in the area, the Germans had begun to make pieced and appliquéd quilts, quickly excelling in a field that was new to them but time-honored amongst their neighbors from the British Isles. It would be several decades before quilts would be as commonplace as the coverlets and feather ticks recorded in local

ESTATE SALE OF
HENRY GILBERT

Centre Township, Snyder County
September 5, 1840

Quilt frame . . . . 13¢

ESTATE INVENTORY OF
JOHN MOORE

Lewisburg, Union County
1840

quilt (patch work) . . . . $ 1.25

ESTATE SALE OF
JAMES McMURTIN

White Deer Township,
. Union County
June 14, 1842

sixteen comfortables from
28¢-$1.00
one quilt at $2.00

ESTATE INVENTORY OF
SARAH MATHER

West Buffalo Township,
Union County
filed November 14, 1842

one quilt . . . . $ 2.00
one comfort . . . . 75¢
three quilts . . . . $ 2.25
three coverlets . . . . $ 6.00
two worsted quilts . . . . $ 1.50

ESTATE INVENTORY OF
JOHN SMITH, INNKEEPER

Middleburg, Snyder County
filed July 2, 1845

five comforts
4 coverlets &
1 quilt $13.00

estate inventories, but quilts were fast becoming the setting where expert needlework as well as design and color sense could be worked out on a grand scale.

Stars, whether they were the eight-pointed *LeMoyne,* or the ubiquitous *Variable Star* formed from a square and triangles, became the favorite image in Central Pennsylvania's pieced quilts, surpassed only in sheer number by the beginner's *Nine Patch.* Notes attached to quilts, such as one written by Catherine Pontius Gemberling on October 19, 1903, attest to the importance that these early hand-worked textiles played in the lives of the families: "Not to be sold out of family This quilt was pieced [sic] by Christena Pontius 75 years or more the black star was her mother's dress probally [sic] the only calico dress she had because they were homemade linen and wool in the winter. She thought in this way she could remember it P.S. in Mifflinburg her fingers lving in the dust. homemade thread"

In spite of the urging of the fashion editor of the most popular women's magazine of the day, *Godey's Lady's Book,* first in 1835 and then repeatedly in the 1850s, the women in this area of Pennsylvania did not take to the fussy English template method for making silk patchwork but rather continued their pieced and appliquéd work in cottons, lavishing a great amount of care and time on the needlework in the white fill-in blocks: pineapples, grapes, sunflowers, a variety of leaves, some stuffed and much stippled work. Although examples exist of early silk mosaics in hexagon or baby block designs, they are few. Whole cloth work (except early white work) as well as central medallion and pieces with applied chintz are missing in the repertoire of this seven-county region although examples of the latter are reported as having been made in Lycoming County. What the area women apparently enjoyed doing most and excelled in were quilt tops organized around blocks of pieced or appliquéd designs.

It was the appliqué patterns, many of them distinctly individual in concept, that flourished in the mid-nineteenth century, and they continued to be made in great numbers until near its close. Red and green calicos placed on a field of white, occasionally accented by touches of yellow, orange, or pink, made up the dominant palette. Those few worked on a solid color field seem out of place and are felt to be examples of isolated occurrence or of a maker recently arrived in the area from the more solidly "Dutch" counties, Dauphin, Berks, or Lancaster. Some of these mid-nineteenth century appliquéd examples were proudly signed and dated by area women: Elizabeth Baer Jordon (b. 1831 in Aaronsburg, Centre County, m. David Shoemaker in 1851) on her *Tulip Wreath* with stuffed work signed "Elizabeth Jordon age 20 March 1851"; Dina Miller (Haines Township, Centre County) made another *Tulip Wreath* which she signed and dated "1853" while still unmarried. Women from the Spyker and Stroehecher families of Lewisburg borough and neighboring East Buffalo Township in Union County signed and dated a group of unassembled appliqué patches between 1854-1867, while Margery Coulter Linn of Buffalo Crossroads, Union County, pieced a large tulip appliqué which was documented by her son in its corner: "June the 12. This quilt was pieced by/Mrs. Margery Linn in the sixty/ninth year of her age in the year fifty/and quilted by Miss McClelland/penned by William T. Linn." The VanDyke women of Nippenose Valley, Lycoming County, made a series of abstract paper cut out appliqué quilts and tops dated "1850" that feature the initials of their large family in counted cross stitch in the center of each of the blocks. These signed and dated appliqués serve as benchmarks in textile dating as well as those that were made by women just prior to their known marriages.

Flower motifs such as the *Whig Rose,* the *Tulip* or *Rose Wreath,* the *Peony* or *Pomegranate,* the *North Carolina Lily,* and the *Cockscomb* were the most popular but they are repeated only as general types, rarely as identical patterns. Most often they were laid out in quadrants but they were also arranged in blocks, sometimes within a rake, and usually with an elaborate border or borders to frame the *tour de force.* The variations on appliquéd patterns were many as was the technical handling. Colors were usually placed beside each other but could be layered on top of each other, done in reverse appliqué and sometimes padded.

Although red and green in calicos and solid fabrics dominated the palette of appliqué work here, it was pink and green that prevailed in pieced work. Starting with some mid-century fabrics, their use reached a crescendo in the last quarter of the nineteenth century when, from the enormous variety of calicos extant in these colors, one would think that textile manufacturers were making little else. Sometimes as many as six different small-figured greens or pinks are scattered throughout a single pieced top. Initially they appear to be the same fabric but on close examination there are minute differences. Other regions of Pennsylvania that have been studied more informally yield an abundance of work in this same palette. It appears to have been an overwhelming favorite which continued in popularity past the turn of the century until fabric prints changed abruptly in the late 1920s and the 1930s. Even appliqués of that late period are often done by area women in solid pastels of pink and green. When asked about the combination, the reply was, "We just like it." Occasionally the

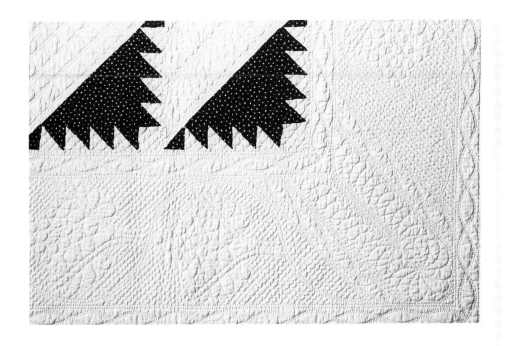

Mifflinburg, Union County. / Pieced calicos on white top with plain back. Applied white binding. 88"×79" with 11 stitches per inch. / Collection of Jane Town Watson.

Quilt by Elizabeth Gebhart Hoy b. 1829 d. 1864 Union County. / Pieced calicos on white top with plain back. Applied white binding. 84"×83" with 8-9 stitches per inch. / Collection of Mr. and Mrs. Millard Boyer.

Quilt by Christena Pontius b. 1785 d. 1877 Mifflinburg, Union County. / Pieced calicos on white top with plain back. Applied white binding. 85"×83" with 12 stitches per inch. / Collection of Linda and Allen Wehr.

A great variety or abundance of quilting patterns are in most of the earliest area quilts. Some of the patterns which are seen in these examples, such as the pineapple on Elizabeth Hoy's Feathered Star, do not exist in later nineteenth century examples here. The stitching on these three examples is very consistent, an indication that one quilter rather than a group worked on these projects; projects which were designed to please the maker as much as anyone else.

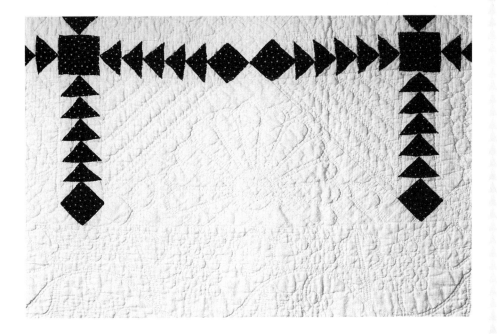

Basted appliqué patches of calico and solid colored fabrics on white top. 23"×22½" and 35"×34" / Collection of Shirley and Robert Kuster.

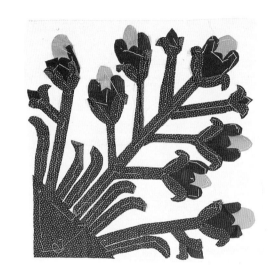

Anna Catherine Zeigler. Courtesy: Linda Wehr.

Quilt top by Hannah Kramer Grove b. 1849 d. 1932 Milesburg, Centre County. / Appliquéd calico and solid colored fabrics. 75"×73" / Collection of Virginia Ulrich.

Quilt top by Anna Catherine Pursel Zeigler b. 1864 Columbia County d. 1941 Kelly Township, Union County. / Appliquéd solid colored fabrics. 64" square / Collection of Mrs. J. S. Zeigler.

Tops, such as these, were often made well in advance of quiltings. Many unassembled patches and even more tops are still found in bureau drawers, suit boxes, and blanket chests. Other quilting paraphernalia such as these forged iron quilting clamps are seen less frequently. They were used to hold together a large frame composed of four long boards with attached muslin strips. Women often preferred the smaller racket-type frames since they took up much less room in the house. Often there were not whole rooms to spare in which to set up the large full-sized frame.

Quilt by Susanne Beahm Meyer b. 1845 d. 1919 Haines Township, Centre County. / Appliquéd calico and solid colored fabrics with some embroidery on white top with striped back. Applied calico binding. 40" square with 7-9 stitches per inch. / Collection of Dr. Paul Meyer Corman.

The crib quilt that Susanne Beahm Meyer made for her second child, Mella Mae b. June 15, 1876, is an example of taking an appliqué design that was usually done in quadruple on a full size quilt and using it singlely and in full scale on a crib quilt. Other examples have been seen which do this in the Cockscomb and the Princess Feather designs, Mrs. Meyer used a limited amount of reverse appliqué. She also quilted a variety of leaves that are integrated with the appliquéd leaves and branches. This subtle and playful technique was done by other area quilters occasionally.

Susanne Beahm Meyer (center) posed in January 1898 with her husband and three children including her daughter, Mella Mae. Photo by Smith of Millheim. Courtesy: Paul Meyer Corman.

Quilt by Catherine Alsbach Heiser m. circa 1840 d. 1892 Buffalo Township, Union County. / Appliquéd solid colored fabrics on white top with plain back. Applied solid colored binding. 70"×68¾" with 7-9 stitches per inch. / Collection of Cherry Will.

This quilt still exhibits its vivid colors unlike many other appliqués of this time which have had their strong greens fade to tans thereby distorting the original vibrancy and the overall effect. The solid blues, greens, yellows, and reds are set against the white background which was lovingly quilted by Catherine with oak leaves, stars, tulips, tear drops, hearts, double hearts, and princess feathers, many of them outlined by double rows of the quilter's running stitch.

Snyder County. / Appliquéd in calicos on white top with applied crocheted lace. 15³/₄" × 15¹/₂" / Collection of Shirley and Robert Kuster.

The only appliquéd or pieced doily found, it is a scaled down rendition of a pattern, called Laurel Leaves, *done in a quilt top of the same period, circa 1850-1870. "Ellen Weaver" is sewn in green thread in counted cross stitch. Very few pieces are signed in any manner: stamped, in ink script, or sewn.*

Penns Creek, Snyder County/Pieced and appliquéd solid colored fabrics on white top with plain back. Applied solid colored binding. 82" square with 8 stitches per inch. / Collection of Shirley and Robert Kuster.

Double row quilting was another approach to needlework in those quilts where the quiltmaker took her time as seen in this Eagle *which has a Pennsylvania-German urn with large geometric flowers along with a variety of leaves, flowers, and hearts. Quilted hearts were found on quite a few areas pieces some of which were said to be wedding quilts by family. Hands were also used as an occasional quilting motif, all three examples seen were of young children. One owned by the Union County Historical Society was made by Mary Jean Shantz of West Buffalo Township in 1898 with the tracing of her three-year-old grandaughter, Clara Reigle's hand, in each corner.*

strong pink and green palette is relieved by the use of orange, red, or even blue fabric or placed on a field of white work. Its use and popularity is hard to avoid, distinctive, and eventually becomes to the initiated, pleasingly strong.

As early as 1876 another phenomenon occurred here: the emergence of the *Eagle* appliqué as a favorite. Often thought by present quilt owners to be unique, it was anything but. Although a printed period source still eludes researchers, it must have existed because of the marked similarity in the eagle's basic body construction and layout and the consistent overall format of the three dozen "unique" quilts seen (see p.34). It was a pattern so popular here, along with the large single *Bethlehem Star,* that it was frequently made again in the 1920s as a copy of "Grandmother's" as in the Heiser family of Heiser Crossroads, Union County, where Matilda Heiser Spiegelmeyer of Buffalo Crossroads made one for each of her grandchildren based on an early example made by her mother, Catherine Alsbach Heiser (married c. 1840). A number of the area's nineteenth-century *Eagle* appliqués had dates from the 1880s sewn in them or show provenance from that period. The earliest known example was a crib quilt by Susanne Beahm Meyer of Coburn, Centre County, for her daughter, Mella Mae who has born in June 1876. The date of Mella's birth lends credence that this pattern was stimulated by the country's centennial or, as Florence Peto maintained in an early article, that it appeared at the time of the Civil War as a patriotic Union quilt.

The intriguing aspect of this group of quilts is how uniformly rigid certain aspects are: the use of the shield as the eagle's torso, the wide-open wing spread, the fan-shaped tail, the very simplistic neck, head and beak, the placement of the four eagles on angle to the quilt's corners, and the use of central concentric circles or wreaths. Other aspects change dramatically from one quilt to the next: the shape and placement of the birds' feet as well as what they carry in their beaks: a basket, cherries, a stuffed cherry, a ring, a leaf, or stick. The quilting on all but two of the examples is fairly rudimentary with the overall appliqué design appearing to dominate the piece. Several exhibit some invention with scalloped quilting read as feathers.

In stylistic contrast to the abundant but straightforward pieced stars, nine patches and flying geese of cottons were the crazy quilts of silks, velvets, and wools dating from the last quarter of the nineteenth century. As Virginia Gunn noted in her recent paper on late nineteenth-century embroidered work in *Uncoverings* (1985), a handicraft craze that had started as early as the 1860s in England under the tutelage of John Ruskin and William Morris, exploded upon the American scene in the late 1870s and 1880s. Central Pennsylvanians got caught up in the fervor although sometimes in a more subdued manner and never at the expense of their simpler cotton pieced and appliquéd traditions.

Announcements of this new "artistic" home decorating trend appeared first in editorials of the ladies' magazines in 1879, followed by articles which called them the new Japanese inspired quilts or "crazies." By 1884 they were an important part of the popular magazines such as *Godey's, Peterson's,* and *The Delineator.* Instructions, examples, and advertisements for the purchase of appropriate sample fabrics appeared in abundance. Crazy quilts were part of the overall trend toward fancy or artistic work and were executed in our area simultaneously with patterns from an earlier simpler era. Many of the area's crazy quilts have dates sewn in them. The high style silk

Quilt by Elizabeth Baer Jordon Shoemaker b. 1831 Aaronsburg, Centre County d. circa 1903 Lock Haven, Clinton County. / Appliquéd calicos on white top with plain back, dated "1851." Applied calico binding. 84"×83" with 8 stitches per inch. / Collection of Mrs. Margaret S. Thomas.

Elizabeth Jordon's signed and dated quilt is one of two found in the area with areas of white stuffed work sometimes called trapunto: large petaled flowers, princess feathers, and swirling swasticas in addition to the frame around her name and date: "Elizabeth Jordon 1851." The rows of quilting that surround the stuffed designs are as close as ¹/₄" and further accentuate the puffed effect. The piece was made for her hope chest and it was shortly after its completion that she married David Otto Shoemaker of Bedford County.

Elizabeth Baer Jordon Shoemaker. Courtesy: Mrs. Magaret S. Thomas.

examples are those often dated from the mid- to late 1880s with one made as late as 1935. Most were made in a combination of fancy dress fabrics, ribbons, ties, hat linings, and velvets, which sometimes came from a local casket company, seamstress or milliner. A large number were made solely of wool, one of suit sample swatches, while only one was made of cottons.

As late as June 1899, the A. C. Importing Company of Beaver Springs, Snyder County, advertised in *The Designer* that for twenty-five cents a mammoth package would be sent of over one hundred silk remnants, some over thirty inches square, in addition to pattern instructions for sixty crazy stitches. The great number of companies selling such fabric scraps (as many as six on one page of *The Ladies' Home Journal* in February 1884) indicate that this type of quilt was not so much the mirror of one's own dress fabrics as other pieced quilts.

Area crazy quilts can be divided into two basic types. The silk or velvet covers were often without filling. On them local women lovingly wrought a great variety and abundance of fancy stitches, sewed sequins and beads, and embroidered or painted scenes and motifs promoted by *Godey's, Peterson's,* and *Arthur's.* Much simpler wool examples were usually decorated with a single fancy stitch in wool, often in one unifying color such as yellow or red, as advocated by the more practical periodicals such as *The National Stockman and Farmer* or *Good Housekeeping.* Sometimes they might have sewn or painted surface designs as well.

Both types were done in an overall random effect but were made most often by assembling a series of blocks. Some were done in pieced block designs reminiscent of the earlier pieced cotton tradition: the *Dresden Plate, Robbing Peter to Pay Paul,* as well as the *Fan,* described in detail by Jane Weaver for *Peterson's* (January 1885, p. 86).

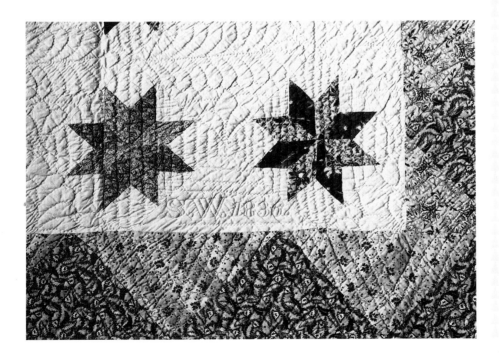

Quilt by Sarah Wilson b. 1788 New Hanover Township, Montgomery County d. 1872 New Berlin, Union County. / Pieced chintz and calicos with plain back, dated "1836." Applied white binding. 104¹/₂"×101¹/₂" with 8 stitches per inch. / Collection of Mary Wilson Boyer Laign.

Quilt by Alice Walter b. 1867 d. 1927
Swengel, Union County. / Pieced wools and
satins with plain back with various colors
and stitches in embroidery floss. Applied
solid colored binding. 68″×66″ with 6-7
stitches per inch. / Collection of Pauline
Showalter Miller.

This is a good example of an ordered
crazy quilt based on a series of blocks and
a central medallion. Numerous ordered
crazies have been seen here using patterns
like the Bull's Eye, Dresden Plate, or Fan.

Alice Walter taken by J.C. Slear of
Mifflinburg. Courtesy: Pauline
Showalter Miller.

*T*his design of Fans, for patchwork, is something entirely new, and certainly produces the most charming effect for patchwork we have ever seen. We give two cuts of it. It is to be made upon a foundation of soft muslin, and the blocks must be perfect squares. Mark off, upon the foundation-block, the size and shape of the pieces composing the fan. The lower part, answering to the sticks of the fan, is in one solid piece. After the design is marked off, begin at the left side, baste on the small side-piece, allowing enough for the seam of the next piece to cover it. Then take the next piece, run it down on the wrong side, turn it over, and baste it into place. Proceed in this manner until all the pieces are on, then put on the lower or stick pieces, then the upper part of the block, which must always be black, either satin or silk. The stick part looks best of velvet, of some light color. Cover all the seams with feather-stitch embroidery in gold-colored embroidery-silk. Work simple designs in the different sections. Some may be painted, instead of embroidered. We gave a diagram showing how the blocks are to be put together. All seams are to be covered with the feather-stitch. Any variety of embroidery-silks may be used with advantage, and great taste and ingenuity may be brought into requisition to produce good effects of color and variety of design. The colors are marked, though others may be used.

*"Fan Design for Patchwork Quilt,"
by Mrs. Jane Weaver /
Petersons January 1885 / pp.86-88*

Excerpts from the Estate Inventory of Molly Fisher, Penns Township, Snyder County, filed January 15, 1850

A true and perfect inventory, and Just appraisment of all and singular the goods and chattels, rights and credits, which were of Molly Fisher, late of the Township of Penns, county of Union, in the state of Pennsylvania, deceased, at the time of her death, viz:

	$	cts.
2 Quilts	2	50
1 Quilt & Bed case & one Blanket	1	00
7 Yds of cloth at $3. per Yd.	21	00
1 Sewing Basket & Sundries		12 1/2
Remnants of Calicoes		25
2 Yds. Blue calico		20
5 Muslin		62 1/2
A lot of calico, checks, & nankeen		37 1/4
2 Pair of Scissors & Specks		12 1/2
2 Paper Boxes with Thread		10
A Lot of Muslin & patches		12 1/2
A Lot of Patches & Thread		25
6 Yds Muslin		36
A Lot of Patch work & Trunk	1	00
A Lot of old cloth		50
1 Chaf Bag & old cloth		25
2 Ladies Basket		12 1/2
A Lot of Flax, cotton, & Woolen yarn	2	00
5 Patched Quilts	3	50
2 Quilts & one Table cloth	3	75
3 old cloths		12 1/2
A Lot of cotton laps & woolen yarn		62 1/2
2 lbs. Bees wax		40
1 set of Quilting frames		12 1/2
1 Loom		06

Penns Twp. 1/15/1850

REMNANTS

SADIE'S SILKEN SHOWER OF SATIN SAMPLES

The Delineator, *December 1892*

Quilt by Bucknell students, Lewisburg, Union County. / Pieced silks, velvets and cottons with machine stitched backing. Applied solid colored binding. 76¾"×63½" with a various colors and stitches in embroidery floss. / Collection of Catherine K. Stahl.

This fundraising quilt was made by Bucknell students from the class of 1896 and 1898 in support of the Vincent Chapel in Chillisquaque, Northumberland. The Chapel was non-denominational and named for Bishop Vincent who lived there and who gave money toward its construction. Bucknell students were in charge of the services and they were paid two dollars plus an evening meal per Sunday as late as the 1920s. The lamb of Christ, hearts, stars, and horseshoes are among the images stitched into the quilt's top along with Bucknell's colors.

Quilt by Margaret Evans Strohm b. circa 1855 Spring Mills, Centre County d. 1939 in Scranton, Lackawanna County. / Pieced silks and velvets with plain back with various colored threads and stitches in embroidery floss, dated "1885" and "1888." Applied solid colored binding. 65"×64" / Collection of the Centre County Library and Historical Museum.

While Margaret Evans Strohm was living in Centre Hall, Centre County she made this busy crazy quilt that is covered with typical period motifs such as spider webs, umbrellas, a knife and fork as well as a musical scale.

Many of the wool crazies were filled with a thick layer of wool and most, though not all, were knotted (tied) together. Locally they were called "haps," a term that is commonly understood to be synonymous with a comfort or comfortable. It is a term not heard in many areas of the country even where they were made, except as recorded recently by Texas quilt historians. At first the word was assumed to be Pennsylvania German but it is an northern English dialect word meaning a covering of any kind "but generally one applied to one of coarse material," according to the unabridged edition of *The Oxford English Dictionary*. In a survey of mid-nineteenth-century estate inventories of Union County residents, bedding types were listed explicitly and comforts or comfortables were often among those recorded. Simon Hartman's auction in Lewis Township on December 31, 1857 calls them by their colloquial term: "four coverlids at $4.00, and to the widow: three quilts at $1.00 along with seven haps at $3.50, four feather beds at $4.00 and four chaff bags at $2.00." Michael Oberlin's estate also called his comforts "haps" when his inventory was taken at his Hartley Township home in 1852: "one coverlid at $2.00 and two haps for fifty cents."

Pressed work, sewn on foundation and commonly called "Log Cabin" quilts, were never listed as a specific type in estate auctions but they were a popular though less common bedcovering judging from those examples still in area homes. They were made of all silk, all cotton, or all wool during the second half of the nineteenth century, most often in the *Barn Raising* or *Court House Steps* arrangement of light and dark shades. *Furrows* and *Pineapple* patterns also were made by area seamstresses but with far less frequency. A few of the *Log Cabins* were made in smaller crib-sized versions with their individual strips proportionately narrow and fine.

While national arbiters of taste such as Frank Leslie and Candice Wheeler turned their backs on the traditional pieced quilts in favor of what they felt was more original and creative, Central Pennsylvanians did not. Pieced cotton quilts were

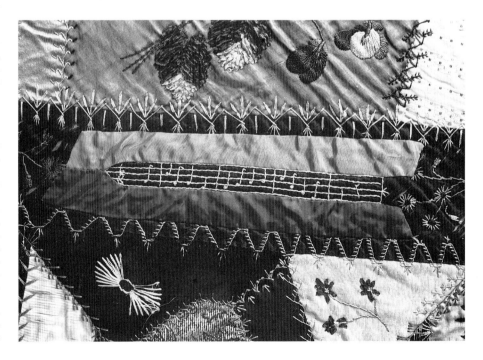

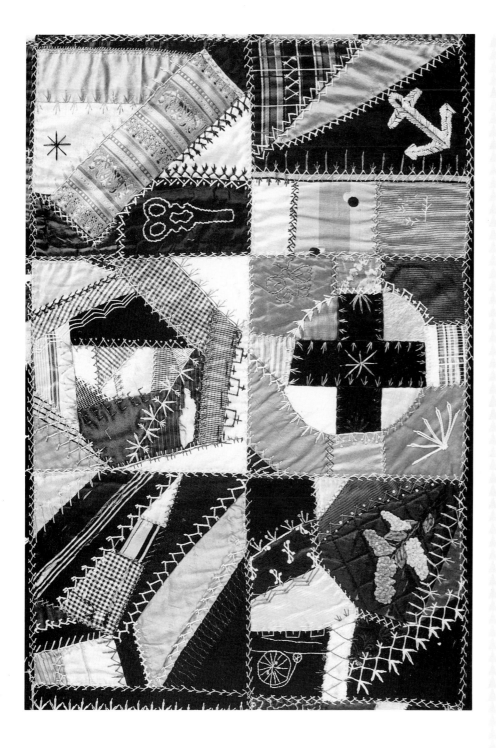

Quilt by Mary Amanda Meyer Losch
b. 1851 d. 1912 and Margaret Emma
Meyer b. 1853 d. 1943, Perryville,
Lycoming County. / Pieced ribbons, velvets,
and silks with various colors and stitches
in embroidery floss. Back turned over to
front as edge treatment. 70"×57½" /
Collection of Margaret Mark.

Margaret E. Meyer taken by F.A. Allen
Studio of Williamsport. Courtesy:
Margaret Mark.

Mary A. Losch (upper right) with her
mother, son, and grandson. Courtesy:
Margaret Mark.

The Ladies' Home Journal, *July 1887*

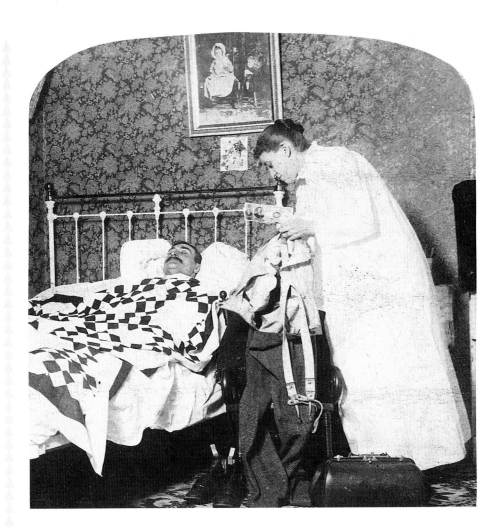

Q̇uilts and comforts keep best hung over poles. Fasten wooden curtain poles stoutly so as to stand a foot from the wall. Space permitting, have them of full comfort length. Several may be set between ceiling and floor, the lowest coming a little less than waist high. Spread quilts and comforts evenly across the poles, one on another, and cover the mass with a sheet of unbleached muslin reaching well below the lowest edges.

Good Housekeeping / *May 1903 / p. 430*

WASHING A COLOURED QUILT.— Make; in a very large tub, a suds of brown soap and water that is not very warm; adding a small tea-cupful of ox-gall to set the colours of the calico. Put in the quilt, and wash it well. Afterwards wash it through a second suds, and wring it very dry. Then rinse it through three cold waters, wringing it very hard out of the last. Hang it immediately out to dry, with the wrong side outwards. An hour or two before evening, turn the right side out. Take it in at sunset, and fold it up. Next morning, hang it out again; as one day (even in summer) is not sufficient to dry a quilt thoroughly, the cotton with which it is stuffed remaining damp a long time in the inside. Towards the end of the second day bring it in, fold it up, and (if it is perfectly dry) put it away. A quilt cannot be ironed. It is best to wash them late in the spring, when they are no longer required for the beds; they will then be ready for the cold weather.

The House Book, *by Eliza Leslie / 1846 / p. 311*

produced simultaneously with the ornate and simple crazy quilts and often by the same women. The magazines that were read here named, as early as 1882, some of the popular pieced patterns:

Lover's Puzzle, Rising Sun, Irish Chain, Joseph's Coat, The Odd Fellow, Old Maid's Ramble, Road to California and Back, King's Crown, Castle Stairs, Moon and Stars, Devil's Puzzle, Robbing Peter to Pay Paul, Pincushion and Cucumbers, Centennial, Bear Paw, Wheel of Fortune, Wedding Knot, Mother's Fancy, Hit and Miss, Toad in Puddle, Texas Tears, Ocean Wave, Brick Wall, Hearts and Gizzards, and *Tangled Garter.*

The fabrics seen in these pieced cotton quilts, documented or thought to have been made from c. 1865 until c. 1920, exhibit a repetitiveness of fabric samples that is at times overwhelming. As Patsy and Myron Orlofsky observed in their landmark text, *Quilts in America* (1974), small print calicos were the mainstay of the American quilt palette and "there are also identical patterns that have been reproduced over a period of sixty or seventy years, which can make dating a quilt by them a guessing game." This certainly was true here. Green print fabric identical to that seen in a signed and dated "1857" quilt, illustrated in Sandi Fox's *19th Century American Patchwork Quilt* (1983), appears repeatedly in our most typical cotton examples and as late as the 1920s. As noted earlier in discussing pink and green calicos, the minute changes exhibited in similar looking fabrics were phenomenal and existed to a lesser extent in the yellows.

By the 1880s patterns appear to have moved from an oral folk tradition, perhaps with some degree of regionalism, to a national commercial level. *Arthur's* and *Peterson's*, followed by *Good Housekeeping, The American Agriculturalist,* and *The National Stockman and Farmer,* began an exchange of pattern names and designs which reached new heights with the formation of The Ladies' Art Company by a German immigrant family in St. Louis, Missouri. Starting off with approximately three hundred pattern designs, which could be ordered by name and number, they had collected well over five hundred when they stopped publishing in 1928. The homogenization of American quilt traditions had begun. The solitary remote quiltmaker, pictured as untouched by national trends, would become an oddity if not an anachronism.

Coinciding with this broad-based mixing of traditions was the popularization of grandmother's quilt as part of the colonial "revival" movement. Again, publication in women's magazines helped spread the new trend. Prose and poetry selections starting

The backing on these two quilts is late nineteenth century material that simulated pieced fabrics. The Diamond in the Square variation and the LeMoyne Star were both fairly common pieced quilt patterns. When printed this way, on whole cloth, they are called "cheater cloths," which were made first in England mid-century and then in the States. Today it is produced for lazy quiltmakers, who no longer piece their patterns. The back on the left, with its scalloped edge belongs, to a Log Cabin quilt made by mother and daughter, Eliza Hendricks Aurandt and Clara Aurandt, in Kreamer, Snyder County before Clara's marriage in 1889. The fabrics they chose for the top's border and edge binding, as well as the back, are all atypical. Collection of Edna May Aucker (left), Mary Anna and Jack Whalen (right).

in the late 1880s stressed the importance of grandmother's quilt in the home, and in October 1894 Sybil Lanigen in *The Ladies' Home Journal* finally used the word "revival." In her article on pieced designs she illustrates and labels them simply as "a cradle quilt," "an aesthetic quilt," or "a simple design."

Periodicals of 1896 reflect the variety of activities in quiltmaking with a story of an old fashioned quilting bee in the April issue of *The National Stockman and Farmer* in addition to an article praising the use of small woolen and cotton scraps in crazy patchwork. Emma Elwell noted that city dwellers were now attracted to simple pieced cotton quilts and she gave twelve generic patterns for them to copy in the November *Ladies' Home Journal,* while Jane Benson in the same publication advocated the purchasing of good, dye-fast materials instead of using any old scrap in quilts. From January to November, *The American Agriculturalist* published dozens of quilting patterns and patches sent in by their readers as well as a reproduction of Abbot Graves' painting, "Labor of Love," which showed a man quilting. Reader response would keep this exchange of quilt information in full swing well past the turn of the century.

In Helen Blair's article "Dower Chest Treasures" in *House Beautiful* (February 1904) she restates the case for colonial revival in simple pieced cotton quilts as being the answer to Ruskin and Morris's earlier call for handiwork as a means of expressing one's artistic feelings and as a response to the era of "factory mades":

Anna Eliza Hendricks and William Aurandt and their children Clara and George Aurandt taken by Ulrich Studio in Selinsgrove prior to 1889. Courtesy: Edna May Aucker.

. . . the arts-and-crafts movement has given dignity to even the humbler handicrafts. Our artistic ideals are shifting, and fortunately in the right direction. . . . The old quilts which are reappearing under such interesting circumstances are many of them, quite worthy of their recall to consequence. The colors are often the old hand dyes, the patterns marvels of design, and the quilting intricately beautiful. One of these old quilts, into which a woman of long ago put so much creative and adaptive skill, will give an air to even the most commonplace of modern beds. It will glorify a beautiful old bed. If, however one has not preserved the work of some piecing and quilting ancestress, she may, 'an' it please her,' fall herself a piecing. Many of the quilts seen to-day are fresh from the quilter's frame. Beautiful patterns and color effects are easily achieved. There is almost no limit to choice in design and color, but modern taste and requirements will probably incline towards the simpler effects.

Blair's initial articles on colonial revival were followed by subsequent ones by herself and others like Mabel Tuke Priestman in *The Designer* and Anne Orr in *Good Housekeeping.* The revival they advocated was not only seen in quilts but also in household furniture and in architectural design.

Middleburg, Snyder County. / Pieced calicos with print back. Applied calico binding. 91" × 88" with 8 stitches per inch. / Private collection.

The Album *pieced block was a favorite of area quiltmakers. This is one of two to have a stamped design in the centermost piece of each block. In both quilts the stamped design, as seen here, incorporates either male or female names.*

Quilt top by Anna Mary Walker Shutt Hettinger b. 1843 Saulsburg, Huntingdon County d. 1906 Harris Township, Centre County. / Pieced prints and solid colored fabrics, dated "1897." 79" × 66" / Collection of Gloria Braun.

Thirty different pieced blocks, each signed in ink with a pattern name, were assembled by Mary Hettinger while she was living in Pine Grove Mills, Centre County. She signed her pattern "Basket M. Hettinger/March the 18th 1897." Other blocks include Tree of Paradise, Livonia Choice, White House Step, Coffen, Roling Star, *and* Sugar Bole. *One block is signed "Album Quilt February the 22 1897" and it surely is that—one of only a handful seen in this central Pennsylvania area.*

ESTATE INVENTORY OF
DAVID LINN

Kelly Township, Union County
September 6, 1848

2 quilts	$10.00
3 quilts	$18.00
4 quilts	$25.00
3 coverlets	
1 comfort	
9 blankets	$37.00
3 coverlets	
1 comfort	
6 blankets	$24.00
3 coverlets	
1 comfort	
5 blankets	$23.00
6 coverlets	$12.00
9 flannel sheets	$13.50

Margery Coulter Linn b. 1781 d. 1865 Buffalo Crossroads, Union County. / Appliquéd calico fabrics on white top with plain back, dated "1850." Applied calico binding. 97" × 95" with 8-10 stitches per inch. / Collection of Mrs. Linn Kieffer Sr.

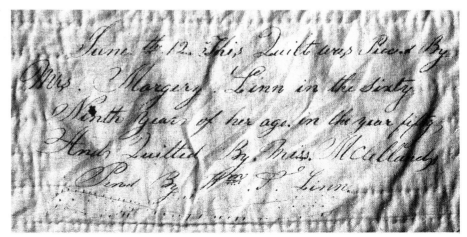

22

Sears executives, E.J. Condon and G.B. Vidal, examine the needlework of quilts that had arrived in Chicago at the time of Sears 1933 Century of Progress Quilt Contest. Courtesy: Sears, Roebuck, Company.

Developing alongside this reappearance and copying of traditional cotton piecework was the emergence of newly designed quilts, as evidenced in a series by *The Ladies' Home Journal* in 1905. The simple outline embroidered quilts, usually of white background with red thread, also became a major fad from this time well into the 1920s. The popularity of new designs was the more erratic of these two trends.

Those quilts designed for *The Journal* by Maxfield Parrish, Peter Newell, and Jessie Wilcox Smith among others, have been seen only on the printed page but they may have served as a liberating influence by suggesting that other people's new designs were as valid a statement as the repetition of old motifs. This trend is illustrated in a series of new patterns to come out of the Midwest in particular and the mix of new as well as oldtime favorites on the batting wrappers of Mountain Mist. New designs were also judged as a separate but equal category in the 1933 Sears, Roebuck national quilt competition. As seen in dozens of Central Pennsylvania quilts, women here were attracted to the new patterns such as *Daffodils, Iris,* and *Sweet Pea* in addition to creating their own adaptations.

Mrs. George R. Leitzel of Northumberland gained second place with an original design in one of ten regional contests sponsored by Sears in their contest, "A Century of Progress 1833-1933." Mrs. Leitzel's pieced and appliquéd quilt illustrated a Conestoga Wagon drawn by six horses and driver with the inscription "Philadelphia to Pittsburgh in twenty days" and contrasted it with an airplane circling the globe with the embroidered saying, "Around the world in less than nine days!" It won in a competition with 1700 quilts from Pennsylvania, New York, New Jersey, and West Virginia. Her quilt, along with the first and third prize winners from the Philadelphia district was given a cash award and was sent on to the Sears building at the World's Fair in Chicago where it competed for the grand prize of one thousand dollars.

The publicity of this contest celebrating Sears' centennial, and the 24,878 quilts submitted, along with the promotions of Stearns and Foster's Mountain Mist wrappers, pattern pamphlets put out by Aunt Martha, Virginia Snow, and Grandmother Clark, as well as magazine and newspaper coverage of quilt patterns, made quiltmaking extremely fashionable throughout the 1930s. Terms like "homey," "old fashioned," "grandmother's," encouraged the proliferation of traditional patterns to the point that the *National Stockman's* editors wondered if the revival had not gotten out of hand, and Carlie Sexton disdainfully called them "reproductions" in 1924. Sears, on the other hand, encouraged the rethinking of quiltmaking by offering a bonus of two hundred dollars if the winner of their contest turned out to be one who had designed

Women of Colonial times have left many delightful specimens of quilt making which are being carefully preserved as precious heirlooms. You, today, may make for your descendants heirlooms with the modern patterns on this page. A new idea is to have the design on the quilt match the bedside rug, and two of these matching rugs on this page are cross-stitched with bias-fold tape. There is a woman in Kentucky, with sixty mountain women working under her direction, who will do your quilting. Their work is exquisite. Write to Anne Orr for prices. We are offering eight pages of quilt designs, four in full color, two Hot-Iron Transfer Patterns for appliquéd quilts, cutting patterns for eleven pieced quilts, a large sheet of charming quilting patterns, including those shown on this page, all in Set 100; 75¢

Good Housekeeping *January 1932 / p.104*

In the last few years quilt-making has revived, not as a necessity, but again taking its place among the fine arts. Everywhere one sees groups of women making quilts, joyous old time neighborliness is again binding our women together. Patterns are exchanged, notes compared and materials traded. And so to this growing neighborliness we dedicate this book . . . . MAKE A QUILT!!!

Sears Century of Progress in Quilt Making *1934 / p.4*

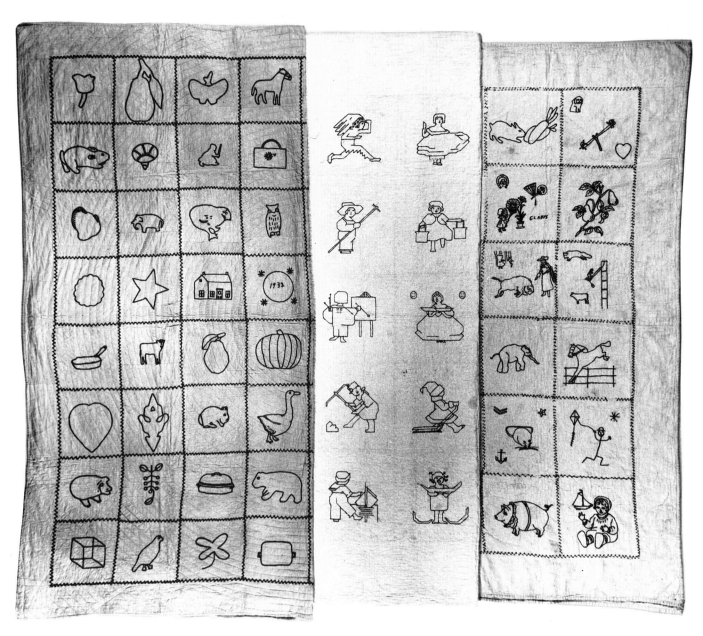

Quilt by Mary Snyder Mader b. 1864 d. 1951 Mifflingburg, Union County. / Embroidered on white top with plain back, dated "1932." 75½"×73½" with machine quilting. / Collection of Lou Jane and James Mitchell.

Quilt by Helen Kerstetter b. 1915, Blaine, Perry County. / Embroidered on white top with plain back. Front to back as edge treatment. 69½"×59½" with 6-8 stitches per inch. / Collection of Helen Arlene Kerstetter.

Quilt by Gladys Dunkelberger Crone b. 1909 Trevorton, Northumberland County d. 1980 Elysburg, Northumberland County. / Embroidered on white top with plain back, dated "1927." 70" square with 8-9 stitches per inch. / Collection of Donna Crone.

Dates from 1894 to 1932 were found on the quilts of this type: white whole cloth with images outlined in red thread. Nearly five dozen were seen—doll quilts, crib quilts, full-sized examples such as these three—indeed, they appeared to have been a favorite type of bed covering at that time. Mary Mader's top is unusual in that the images are fairly abstract personal renderings of familiar household objects such as a griddle, an escutcheon, a side table, and the menacing lady from the Old Dutch Cleanser can. Arlene Kerstetter's quilt is made of transfer patterns she ordered as a youngster from Child Life magazine, each image representing a state such as the watermelon eating girl from Alabama. Many area women remember purchasing stamped muslin squares at their local dry goods store for pennies apiece but they could cost as much as 35¢. Some of those are seen on Gladys Dunkelberger's quilt, personalized by the addition of a family pet's name such as "Jack," "Taby" or "Topsy" or that of a sibling or friend: "Jean," "Sara," "Albert," "Russell," and "Fern." Other of her squares are distinctly amateurish and even juvenile with stick figures. The combination of what was commercially available along with personal drawings is unusual.

Mary S. Mader. Courtesy: Mary Arnold / Helen Kerstetter. Courtesy: Helen Arlene Kerstetter. / Gladys Dunkelberger. Courtesy: Donna Crone.

her own along the "Century of Progress" theme. Co-existing with these two trends was the simple embroidered quilt.

Dozens of examples from 1894-1932, some of them designed as fundraisers, have turned up in our area. Their sewn outline images hark back to the transfer outfits advertised in the 1880s for dresser scarfs, pillows, and throws, which were used on many crazy quilt surfaces. At that time they were transferred on the material either to be filled in with elaborate varied stitching including chenille work, or outlined in a simple running stitch but in a variety of colors and thread types. These embroidered narrative illustrations, many of them Kate Greenaway's, when on dresser scarfs, were quite often sewn only in red thread, a trend which became common in quilts made after the turn of the century.

Many of the older owners of quilts of this period remember buying for a few pennies at the local dry goods store the blocks with their designs already stamped on them, sometimes as Gretchen Royer of Williamsport did, on their weekly excursion to town. They might be advertised as a series of designs in a children's magazine complete with educational inscriptions or one could add one's own. Often they were somewhat detailed in their rendering of favorite animals, stories, or familiar objects. They stood out vividly from their plain muslin backgrounds, when sewn in the familiar Turkey red thread which withstood repeated washings. Sometimes they were rendered in blue or in mixed colors.

Also executed, most often in the red on a white background, were local fundraising quilts. People paid to have their names stitched on the quilts. Usually the quilts would be raffled or sold when finished, thereby generating additional income. Or, they might be given to the quiltmaker or a local minister. As Dorothy Cozart indicated in her recent paper on 49 fundraising quilts in *Uncoverings* (1985), from two to fifty cents might be raised through each signature, depending on placement. Two quilts she studied actually showed in stitching the amount raised. Usually twenty-five to one hundred dollars, but sometimes much more, was thus raised for a worthy cause. A couple of the Central Pennsylvanian examples of this type were done by community women to raise funds for the Red Cross in World War I but most were done by church groups: The Ray's Church in Limestone Township in 1897, the Mazeppa Evangelical Church in 1926, the Grace Evangelical United Church in York in 1918, the Flemington Methodist Evangelical Church in 1927, and the Sunday School of the Methodist Evangelical Church in Williamsport for example. Some were pieced cotton designs: stars, crosses, bricks, even a *Drunkard's Path*, while others were strictly embroidered motifs, often spoked wheels. Most were similar to those seen by Mrs. Cozart in that they had from 150-400 names each. One had a Christmas message to Reverend and Mrs. Harvey Crow stitched in by the Ladies' Aid Society of the Mt. Bethel Reformed Church in Clinton County.

For those who had not been taught to piece by a relative or friend, instructions began to be very explicit on color use in the early twentieth century. If one lacked

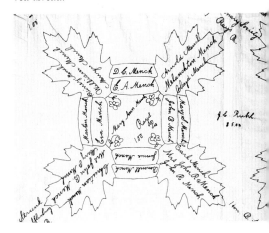

Hartley Township, Union County. / Embroidered on white top, dated "1897." 83" square. / Collection of Helen Ruhl Kerstetter.

Five hundred and fifty-one names of adults and children were solicited by members of the St. Peter's Aid and Missionary Society of the Ray's Lutheran Church for this fundraising quilt top. Each person paid one dollar and a few paid five dollars in order that theirs be included. When completed, the piece was auctioned off and bought for one hundred dollars by Jeanne Reish Frederick, grandmother of the present owner and herself a quilter. Names like Mench, Eberhart, Hudson, Dale, Ruhl, Morningstar, Boop, Zimmerman, Wagner, and Yohn are sewn in the Turkey red thread.

Snyder County. / Appliquéd solid colored fabric on white top with plain back. Applied white binding. 83"×82" with 8-10 stitches per inch. / Collection of Jean W. Haines.

Between August 1918 and April of the following year, signature pledges at ten cents each were collected by local Red Cross workers in order to raise needed funds. Chances were then sold on the completed quilt which Retta Hughes won at a raffle in 1919. This is one of two area Red Cross fundraising quilts seen, both with red and white appliqué crosses and signatures.

Jane Brouse on her marriage day to Wilson Rothermel on February 14, 1903. Courtesy: Laura E. Latsha.

Sample patches by Jane Brosius Rothermel b. 1877 d. 1936 Washington Township, Northumberland County. Pieced solid colored and print fabrics. Collection of Laura E. Latsha.

These thirty-five patches by Jane Brosius were handed down to her daughter who found names for all but two in period quilt pattern books: Grandmother Clark's, St. Louis, 1931 and Quilt Patterns by the Ladies' Art Company, St. Louis, 1928. Many of them are known by other names as well, a point of confusion and argument in some people's minds. Left page: Wedding Ring, Texas Rose, unidentified, Rose Album, Philadelphia Pavement, Flower Basket, Mosaic #3, Four Tulips, Cherry Basket, Double X and Tree of Paradise. Right page: Four Stars, Hour Glass, Crosses and Losses, Circle or Base Ball, Compass, Dahlia, Odd Fellows, Eight-Point Design, Jacob's Blocks, Aunt Lydia's Star, Morning Star, Maple Leaf, Sunflower, Eight-Point Star, Diamond and Half Diamond, Double X, Double T, and Evening Star.

the skill or the time, patches already cut for a whole quilt could be ordered in 1929 both from the Patchwork Corporation at 233 Fourth Avenue, New York City, for seven and one-half dollars, or for ten to fifteen dollars from the Practical Patchwork Company in Marion, Indiana. Completely finished hand-quilted bedcoverings and pillows also became available, being advertised nationally in *House Beautiful* (January 1929), out of Kirk, Kentucky: $20.25 for a finished crib quilt and $5.25 for a matching pillow. Six months later Mrs. Elanor Beard announced that she had opened stores in New York, Pasadena, Santa Barbara, and Chicago where she would sell quilts designed exclusively by herself at her studio in Hardinsburg, Kentucky, and quilted by "skilled Kentucky needlewomen." It was not long before Fruit of the Loom was offering machine quilted bedspreads which "copied designs of early American patches *(Good Housekeeping,* 1931)." Quiltmaking traditions had undergone many changes from 1830-1930.

*I*n talking at length with seventeen older traditional quilters, most of them born in the first decade of the twentieth century, some observations can be made. These women reminisced about their quiltmaking, often their mother's and sometimes their grandmother's, transporting us to an earlier time. Had we been able to interview their older relatives, the conclusions might have been different however, their responses more complex and in depth.

Most of the women were either quite young—about six years old—or young women—about sixteen—when they first took part in quiltmaking. Most began by actually quilting although some were initiated by knotting a comfort, piecing a small nine-patch, or carding wool for a new comfort. They were taught most often by their mother, sometimes a grandmother, aunt, neighbor, or friend. As Sarah Fiedler from Aaronsburg noted, "Grandmother said, 'You were born for a purpose and it wasn't to fold your hands.' " Most girls of all eras are eager to do what their mothers did as Miriam Seebold of New Berlin noted, "Whatever she had to do, well, I had to do, too!"

With the exception of two of the quilters, the young girls learned and enjoyed doing piece work rather than appliqué. Most of their patterns were obtained through trading with family or neighbor ladies although some had quilt books or pamphlets like Virginia Snow's while a few made their own designs. They enjoyed reading the batting wrappers of Mountain Mist which were influential in determining some of their pattern range starting in the late 1920s. The *Poinsettia* (#39), *Dancing Daffodils* (#24), and *Water Lilies* (#47) were among the women's favorites. Some of the patterns such as the *Bethlehem Star* were especially appreciated since the quilter's past was associated with them. Few of the women remembered seeing a collection of "sample" patches although two extensive family collections and one of a church group have been discovered.

Most of the women said they used whatever materials were handy, some feeling that it was a waste to buy materials for quilts other than what was needed for the back and the fill-in blocks and border. Most used remnants, scraps gathered from dress and shirt making, and stored in drawers or boxes. Some of their

favorite patterns, such as the *Dresden Plate, Wedding Ring, Basket of Scraps,* and *Grandmother's Flower Garden,* were particularly good for using a great variety of scraps. Sometimes good parts of discarded clothing, often wools, were used for crazy quilts made up as comforts. When new material was used, it was most often purchased from Sears, Roebuck and Company, where orders were promptly filled, or a local dry goods store such as J. D. S. Gast and Son, Mifflinburg, Leiser's in Lewisburg, or Cook's in Vicksburg. Sometimes materials were given to a quilter by an uncle who worked at a silk factory, suiting samples by a salesman-neighbor, or by an aunt who was a milliner. As Margaret Seebold from New Berlin observed, "Quilts make you think a little of the person who made it or whose dresses were in there. Maybe you don't think of them any other time except when you see that quilt."

Not many of these women used feedbags or outing flannel for quilt backs. Most did not use silks since they felt they did not wear well, many of their grandmothers' silk crazy quilts already being fragile and torn. They disagreed as to whether percale was desirable, some feeling that it was harder to quilt since it was so tightly woven.

All felt that quilts were among the most colorful items in their homes although carpets, braided rugs, and draperies might be also. Color was considered to be an important aspect of quiltmaking and the quilts to be an outlet for expressing one's color sense. Yet, when the women were asked how they judged others' quilts, needlework and piecing accuracy were always the pre-eminent criteria. Reds and greens as well as pinks and greens, and "bright colors" were cited as favorites. The quilters did not feel that their surroundings specifically influenced their color sense nor did they feel that the names given certain patterns had anything to do with regional, political, or religious themes. Most felt that the names were not important except in helping them identify someone else's quilt in a conversation. While they called some of the more common types by name, others were simply referred to as "grandmother's," "Aunt Lydia's," "the church women's," et cetera.

Consistently they called heavy bed coverings, either knotted or quilted, "comforts," "comfortables," or "haps" and the words were interchangeable. A hap was always thick and heavy. They were often, although not always, filled with wool (sometimes cotton or a worn quilt) and usually knotted. Those that were quilted were done with coarser though even quilting, usually five stitches to the inch. As Sara Reigle from Heiser's Crossroads said, "Comforts are not used as much now that there is heat in the home. When you were under one, you knew it!" Usually the tops of the women's comforts were done in wool in either a random or a planned pattern, and were often connected visually by a "crazy" feather stitch. Yet, some of their comforts were also executed in traditional cotton pieced designs like the *LeMoyne Star* or *Irish Chain.*

Most of the women used purchased Mountain Mist batting for their filler material in their quilts although some used old quilts or sheet blankets which did not puff up as nicely. Many stated that a new quilt should be "all new," including its backing made from good muslin, a sheet, or yardage of apron gingham.

As quilters, the women did not have many superstitions. One *knew* that one did not sew on Ascension Day or lightning would strike. Widely circulated legends found in books concerning a young unmarried woman who quilted her own bridal quilt or who put a heart in one had it that she would become a spinster or again that one needed to have twelve finished quilts as part of the hope chest. Such legends were never heard of or, in the case of the latter, never credited—four or five quilts being the rule here.

New and pleasing quilt blocks which our readers think will interest others and be the means of calling out still other ideas, will be reproduced in these columns from time to time, if desired. Send the cloth pattern itself, pinning the name of the design and your own name and address to it on a slip of paper, and a photograph will be taken, as of the accompanying weeping willow design. If you want the block back, send postage for return. Address the envelope to the Busy Fingers editor, at this office.

American Agriculturalist *March 7, 1896 / p.286*

Perforated patterns can be made practically as perfect as those made by the expensive perforating machines. Take a bit of match about three quarters of an inch long(a) and with a pair of pinchers run the finest size sewing needle (b) lengthwise through the piece of match, letting the point protrude about one quarter of an inch. Then remove the sewing machine needle, and insert this in its place; shorten the stitch and it is ready for work. Put one or more sheets of parchment paper under the design you wish to perforate, pin them at the corner so they will not slip and simply stitch, following the pattern.

"Discoveries," by K.P.G. Good Housekeeping June 1907 / p. 731

When cutting quilt blocks, make a pattern out of a good ink blotter. When placed on the material, it will stick to the goods and not slide around as common paper does.

"Discoveries," by Mrs. C.M., Clinton, Ill., The Designer June 1925.

Tin quilt templates 9¼"-17½" long and 2¾-8" high. Collection of Mr. and Mrs. Eugene A. Charles and the Pennsylvania Farm Museum.

Worn quilts were relegated most often to act as mattress padding or as filler for a comfort, although some saw use in babies' playpens or on sleigh rides.

In quilting, the women all used straight needles usually a #8 "between." One woman broke her needles in by washing them in soap and water so they would not screech. All used their needles until they broke from stress and wear. Size 40 thread was most commonly used although 50 and 60 were others' favorites. In earlier times, before silicone-coated quilter's thread appeared, beeswax was used to coat the thread so it would be less likely to knot. Saliva was used to stop bleeding if one's finger was pricked and alum was used by a few to help toughen the tips of the fingers in anticipation of frequent jagging. Cold water and soap are applied immediately to any blood stains on the quilt, those on the backing or underside sometimes being missed.

With one exception, the sewing machine was not used in any aspect of their quilt projects. The women felt that in piecing by hand, rather than machine, they were able to get neater fitting corners. All were fussy about their stitches as well as those of others, and for this reason most of them felt obliged to look at quilts close up or handheld rather than at a distance. Most did not admit to knowing how many stitches they got to the inch although some mentioned eight to ten; others related how their grandmother or an older neighbor lady used to excel with twelve or thirteen. All felt that it would be nice if their backs were quilted as straight and evenly as the quilt top but that it was not likely. Most quilted along the seams, many on both sides of the pieced seams, and in rows as close, at times, as one-half inch apart. With one exception they quilted toward themselves along lines marked out in pencil and occasionally in chalk or soap. One woman plotted quilting designs on her tops by running them through an unthreaded sewing machine.

The patterns or templates for quilting designs were often found to have been thrown out recently after storage for generations in dresser drawers or suit boxes in the attic. Those like Pearl Coup, of New Columbia, who have kept their templates are particularly proud. Nearly all were made of heavy cardboard and almost exclusively

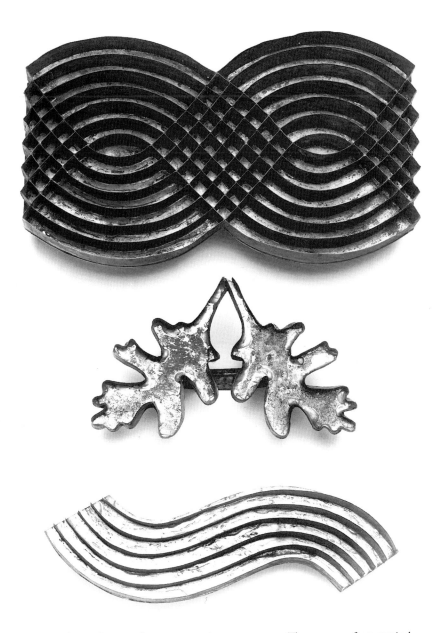

In this design, the pieces of the same shape must be of the same color. The best way to have the sections accurate in shape is to have each separate part cut by a tinman.

Godey's Lady's Book *March 1871 / p.282*

handmade at home by a quilter or sometimes a spouse. They were often copied, drawn off a neighbor's quilt which one admired. Some were of wood, or rubberized roofing material, or tin.

Most of the quilters felt that the quilting should serve more than just the utilitarian function of holding the layers of cloth together. Most felt that each section of the top—mainblocks, sash or rake, fill-in blocks, and/or border(s)—should each be quilted differently and each emphasized in this way. Many had favorite border quilting patterns like a chain or princess feather. A few are now quilting in colored thread in order either to blend with the colors of the fabrics or to emphasize the quilting. Homemade tape completed the edge of their quilts.

Contrary to popular opinion, most of these quilters as well as their older relatives, had quilted alone all their lives or with just one family member or interested neighbor. Although some were now quilting in groups, such as the New Berlin, Laurelton, or Pennsdale women, they were recent exceptions. When group quilting had occurred, it was usually connected with a fundraising event for a church, library or civic organization. Many felt strongly that the results were usually better when one quilted alone. This belief was strongly held by some of the more particular needleworkers.

Most of the quilts were made strictly for use, often as gifts to others or as part of a hope chest or dowry. Few quilted for pay or had heard of many who had or did. Those women whom they remembered as quilting professionally were always paid by the spool, charging between fifty cents and one dollar per spool (or for every two hundred yards). Most charged about two dollars for their work since that was the amount of quilting in an average quilt. Five or six hundred yards of quilting represented truly fine work and one charged accordingly. The women felt strongly that most women quilted for the same reason—the pure joy of it—and often had made more quilts than needed, in effect stockpiling them for the future generations.

Those that remembered an old time quilting bee, whether it was held in a

Quilting template signed on both sides: "October 4th 1868 / Aada Jane Durst / Centre Hall / Centre County, Penna." Courtesy: Louise Reisch.

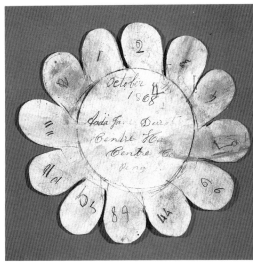

home or a church, recalled that it was an all-day affair attended by six to eight women. The hostess might provide the mid-day meal of pot pie, oyster stew, or pork and sauerkraut, or each might bring their own. Those in attendance were usually related by friendship, proximity or as members of a ladies' aid society. They walked to the bee or were driven in buggies and later cars. Sometimes there were children or men in attendance; children often playing under the quilt frame, which could have been fantasized as a castle or fort, while the men played cards in another room. Everything and anything was the topic of conversation as the quilters worked: recipes were exchanged, taxes, children and the weather discussed, as well as problems pondered. These were social as well as work events and most of the women felt that inferior stitches, unless those done by a learning child, were kept in the piece. Bees stopped being part of their social lives in the 1940s, the period when most of the women felt quiltmaking had reached its low point in general. Card parties and other activities became more important.

Rivalry in needlework, piecing, or design was denied, yet all the women discussed their own and others' work by evaluating how well these different aspects of the quilt were executed. Some noted that inferior quilters and "lefties" were placed at the corners of a quilt frame rather than at its middle or they might be sent out for snacks or on an errand. One woman, who enjoyed the group's gathering but who felt she was not as skilled, participated at her church's quiltings by playing the organ while the others sewed. Grange or regional fairs provided an opportunity for area quilts to be shown and judged, often given recognition by cash or ribbon awards.

Most of the quilters felt that, in general, women tended to quilt for themselves before marriage, having to abandon the craft while their children were being raised. Once the children were all in school, they might be able to return to the quilt frame but this sometimes had to wait until they were grandmothers, quilting then not for themselves but for their grown children or grandchildren. For this reason, many associate quiltmaking traditions with an older generation. Today many of the quilters are making two to four quilts during the winter season while some have begun to quilt year round, freed now from many of the seasonal farm chores.

Quiltmaking appears to have been reserved for bed quilts almost exclusively with only an occasional mention of a pieced and quilted chair back or a sofa cover. Quilted pillows have become a recent rage and many remember and do make smaller quilts for cribs and even doll beds.

Embroidered quilts in Turkey red thread appear to have been the vogue for these women and their mothers in the teens and 1920s, often made as fundraisers for churches. Later construction types such as the cathedral windows and yo-yo quilts were not popular here. Some quilts were especially treasured by a family or individual not because of any particular design or technique (such as appliqué), but rather because of the quilter who made it, for whom it was made, or for other sentimental associations. Most families had quilts they considered special.

Many of the quiltmakers now sign and date their work. This is a fairly recent phenomenon. Few of the old quilts have such sewn documentation although many have come down to the present owners with notes attached as to provenance, and some were specifically mentioned in wills or other formal documents.

Quilts were used in combination with other bedding such as haps and blankets in the wintertime, sometimes as many as three, while summertime use might be limited to one. Many aired and brushed their quilts, only washing them when fairly soiled and sometimes basting a strip of old sheeting at the quilt's upper edge in an effort to keep it from being soiled quickly. As Pearl Coup remarked, "My mother said, 'One washing is worth five year's wear.' " That was obviously a prevailing opinion for quilts were not washed with the frequency they are today.

Rather quilt than "wash dishes," "pick stones," or "sew" these women answer in unison. They strive for perfection in their work, trying not to make stitches so big that a toenail might be caught, but they nod in agreement that probably only God makes things perfect. As Miriam Seebold concludes, "I've gone to quilting and left the lawn go to another day. If you don't go when they (the other quilters) call you, you wouldn't get a smell of it since it goes so fast. I just drop anything and quilt. If there's dust around, just overlook it."

Most quilters feel that today may be the golden age of quilting. Others feel that the 1930s were. In any event they would concur with Miriam Seebold's assessment: "All at once it's like a brush fire. It's really something now!" These quilters and their friends are piecing and quilting more than ever. More women, though not all by any means, made fewer quilts before, while fewer are making more now. In addition, of course many people are wanting to acquire quilts and are looking at them with a renewed intensity. Frames, be they grandmother's, made by dad, bought at an auction, or purchased from Sears, are set up now in bedrooms, living and dining rooms, sometimes the year around.

Post card from the turn of the century depicts a marked quilt in a frame, possibly from the York area. Courtesy: Oral Traditions Project.

"Winnie" at work on her quilt top was one of three photographs taken of her at her home by the Shempp Studio of Williamsport circa 1890. From the Russell and Mary Koch Search estate in Lewisburg. Courtesy: Shirley and Robert Kuster.

W*hen quilting I put court-plaster on the ends of my fingers, renewing it as it becomes pricked through. You'll be surprised how this saves the fingers.*

"Discoveries," by J.R., Cassopolis, Mich., The Designer *August 1923.*

Quilt made for Harriet Maize b. 1831 d. 1877 New Berlin, Union County. / Appliquéd solid colored and calico fabrics on white top with plain back. Applied solid colored binding. 87" square with 12-13 stitches per inch. / Collection of Erma K. Boyer.

This Tulip Wreath, *another favorite regional appliqué pattern, was made for Harriet Maize who died a spinster. She gave the quilt to her sister with instructions that it stay in the Maize family. The pencil marks are still strong, the quilt not having been washed, and they serve to emphasize its abundant and fine quilting. The quiltmaker has been imaginative in quilting the princess feather motif so that it ran along the appliquéd green stem and read both as the familiar quilting pattern and also as leaves. She has also quilted single leaves on the tulip wreaths that repeat their appliquéd counterparts. Her white expanses are filled with the princess wreath, another favorite of area women. The quilt is one of the best organized both in its appliqué work and quilting.*

Quilt by Harriet Hull Pensyl b. 1838 d. 1898 Elysburg, Northumberland County. / Pieced and appliquéd solid colored fabrics with some padded work on white top with plain back. Applied solid colored binding. 86"×87" with 7-9 stitches per inch. / Collection of John and Melodie Persing .

Quilt by Mary Jane Reish Ruhl Frederick b. 1852 d. 1931 Mifflinburg, Union County. / Appliquéd solid colored and calico fabrics on white top with plain back. Applied solid colored binding. 82³/₄" × 80³/₄" with 9-10 stitches per inch. / Collection of Helen Ruhl Kerstetter.

*T*his portfolio of area quilts is arranged so that it illustrates the
following issues in this order: the dominant palette of appliqué and pieced quilts;
the most popular pieced images—stars, geese, and nine patches; the crazy
quilt era, the red embroidered fundraisers and lastly, the palette and
images of the 1930s.

The word came into English from Old French *cuilte*. This is derived from Latin *culcitra*, a stuffed mattress or cushion. From the form *culcitra* came Old French *cotra*, or *coutre* whence *coutre pointe;* this was corrupted into counterpoint, which in turn was changed to counterpane. The word 'pane' is also from the Latin *pannus*, a piece of cloth. Thus 'counterpane,' a coverlet for a bed, and 'quilt' are by origin the same word.

Broadly speaking, from these definitions, any article made up with an interlining may be called a quilt. However, usage has restricted the meaning of the word until now it is applied to a single form of bed covering. In the United States the distinction has been carried even farther and a quilt is understood to be a lightweight, closely stitched bedcover. When made thicker, and consequently warmer, it is called a 'comfort.'
Quilts / Their Story & How To Make Them, by Marie Webster / 1926 / p. 91

Pennsylvania Dutch quilts are easiest of all to identify. They are usually gaudier in color, bolder and more elaborate in design, pieced oftener than appliquéd and superlative in quilting.

Until the Pioneer period, when New Englander, Pennsylvanian and Southerner met in the settling of the West, quilts had characteristics so local that they could be classified geographically almost as easily as the Yankee twang, the Southern drawl, or the inverted sentence formations of Berks and Lancaster counties in Pennsylvania. Different types of people inhabited these three sections of Colonial America, different in background and outlook and hence widely different in habits of thought, whether expressed in words or handicraft.
Old Patchwork Quilts and the Women Who Made Them, by Ruth Findley / 1929 / p. 39

Only a soul in desperate need of nervous outlet could have conceived and executed . . . the ''Full Blown Tulip'' (which she illustrates), a quilt of Pennsylvania Dutch origin. It is a perfect accomplishment from a needlework standpoint yet hideous. The ''tulip'' block is composed of eight arrow-shaped patches of brilliant purplish red; the eight petal-shaped patches inserted between the red arrows are a sickly lemon yellow. The center

Penns Creek, Snyder County. / Pieced and appliquéd solid colored fabrics on white top with plain back. Applied solid colored binding. 82" square with 8 stitches per inch. / Collection of Shirley and Robert Kuster.

This eagle appliqué is typical of most of those seen in the Union/Snyder/Clinton/ Centre County area with its concentric serrated circles, 4 eagles of uniform body type and appliquéd stars. On the other hand, the edge treatment is unusual with its curves rather than scallops.

Quilt by Mary Jane Reish Ruhl Frederick b. 1852 d. 1931 Mifflinburg, Union County. / Appliquéd solid colored and calico fabrics on white top with plain back. Applied solid colored binding. 82³/₄″×80³/₄″ with 9-10 stitches per inch. / Collection of Helen Ruhl Kerstetter.

The quilting in Mary Jane's Whig Rose *variation is in rows only ¹/₄-³/₈″ apart. Her parallel rows and small princess feathers were sewn in a very even ten stitches per inch. Three sets of barely identifiable intitials were embroidered in white thread in the center of some flowers: ''E.R.,'' ''J.M.,'' and ''A.M.H.'' while the stems were done in a chain stitch of colored thread. This quilt is part of a long tradition of red and green appliqués also seen in other states such as Ohio and South Carolina starting in the mid-nineteenth century.*

of each tulip is made of the material used for setting the blocks together—homespun of the most terrifying shade of brownish green, beyond question the accident of a private dyepot. . . . The whole is surrounded by a second border . . . of dazzlingly bright orange. The green-red-lemon-orange combination is enough to set a blind man's teeth on edge. . . . And yet as an example of needlework it is a triumph.

Old Patchwork Quilts, and the Women Who Made Them, by Ruth Findley / 1929 / p. 38

Let him kiss me with the kisses of his mouth. For thy love is better than wine. I am the rose of Sharon and the lily of the valleys. As the lily among thorns, so is my love among the daughters. As the apple tree among the trees of the wood, so is my beloved among the sons. I sat under his shadow with great delight and his fruit was sweet to my taste. He brought me to the banqueting house, and his banner over me was love. Stay me with flagons, comfort me with apples; for I am sick with love. His left hand is under my head and his right hand doth embrace me. . . . My beloved is mine and I am his.

Song of Solomon / *Old Testament*

Freeburg, Snyder County. / Pieced and appliquéd calicos on white top with plain back. Applied solid colored binding. 86" square with 8-9 stitches per inch. / Collection of Shirley and Robert Kuster.

The Whig Rose *or* Rose of Sharon *is reputed to have been a popular pattern for bridal quilts. Indeed, of all the appliquéd patterns seen in the seven county region, it was only surpassed in number by the* Eagle *(23) and simple paper cut-out designs (16). This layout is typical although the selection of pink and green calicos rather than green and red, is not. The pink and green calicos were usually reserved for pieced designs, and the green and reds for appliqués. The inner border is formed of triangles which, when placed off center and back to back, form a rickrack effect. This is often done on area quilts but is unusual in that the triangles here are of two different colors rather than one. The quilting on the piece uses designs that are sewn across the appliqué design regardless of its outlines. This is against the rules. Quilting patterns are usually seen as ways to reinforce pieced or appliquéd designs or to complement them, sometimes by sewing contrasting shapes. In this example neither occurs.*

Quilt by Dorcas Stine Rhodes b. 1836 Warriors Mark, Centre County d. 1889 Oliver Township, Centre County. / Appliquéd solid colored and calico fabric on white top with plain back. Front turned to back for edge treatment. 86"×85" with 8-9 stitches per inch. / Private collection.

The Princess Feather *was one of the more popular appliqué patterns in the region with thirteen variations on that theme having been seen. All were executed with four of these large motifs on a solid background usually framed by a sawtooth, rickrack, or band border. Here, the hard-edged swirling feathers are surrounded by a flower/vine border, a favorite of Dorcas Rhodes, which incorporated the large central flower of each princess feather. Like a few of the early quilters, Dorcas Rhodes took appliquéd pieces and incorporated their shapes in the quilt as quilting patterns. Small leaves along the stem and the large princess feathers which fill in between the appliquéd ones are handled in this way in this quilt made for one of her daughters.*

Margery Coulter Linn b. 1781 d. 1865 Buffalo Crossroads, Union County. / Appliquéd calico fabrics on white top with plain back, dated "1850." Applied calico binding. 97"×95" with 8-10 stitches per inch. / Collection of Mrs. Linn Kieffer Sr.

36

Quilt by Maria Ruhl Spigelmeyer. m. circa 1855 d. 1881 Mifflinburg, Union County. / Pieced and appliquéd solid colored fabrics on white top with plain back, dated "1868." Applied white binding with red piping. 78" square with 11-12 stitches per inch. / Collection of Helen Ruhl Kerstetter.

Margery Coulter Linn pieced this large appliqué after the death of her husband David Linn in July 1848. Elizabeth McClelland, her sister quilted it and her nephew, who lived with her in the old stone house in Buffalo Crossroads, penned in the inscription in 1850. Exceptionally large pineapples are quilted in her fill-in blocks. This was a quilting pattern used in the earliest area quilts but which was abandoned as a motif here by the 1860s. The princess feather, a motif used on fine quilts of all eras, fills in the triangular fill-in blocks while parallel lines surround the appliquéd swag border, a design element felt by some to reflect the design influence of the Empire period. Too few were seen here to pass judgement: several from the late 1830s, this one and other from 1850, and several from the 1930s.

1868 is sewn in the very center of this Pomegranate, Love Apple or Peony quilt made for the quilter's daughter, Anna Elizabeth. It is another favorite of the many floral appliqué designs made by area quiltmakers. As in many, it has a pumpkin orange fabric for a third color, yellows being seen next in frequency of use followed by a few with pinks. The use of piping in the edge treatment is rarely seen. Princess feathers of several sizes are quilted alongside the sawtooth border, along the hand-sewn seams of the four main pattern quadrants, and undulate in the main white border.

Maria Ruhl Spigelmeyer, Courtesy: Helen Ruhl Kersetter

Herndon, Northumberland County. /
Appliquéd solid colored fabrics on
white top with plain back.
Front brought to back as edge
treatment. 82½" square with 8-9
stitches per inch. / Collection of
Shirley and Robert Kuster.

Many area appliqués are one-of-a-kind
designs such as this, where princess
feathers, eight-pointed stars, and
baskets of flowers, all typical motifs,
are uniquely arranged. The quilt
exhibits interest in both the lattice work
of the baskets and the five layers of
fabrics in the rose-like flowers. The
quilting is fine but subordinate to the
image which is often the case in quilts
of particularly bold design or of dark
fabrics.

David Allison family quilt, Porter Township, Clinton County. / Appliquéd solid colored and calico fabrics on white top with plain back. Back brought to front as edge treatment. 98" square with 8-9 stitches per inch. / Collection of Centre County Library and Historical Museum.

Catherine Hill Steck and Frederick Steck, Wolfe Township, Lycoming County. / Appliquéd calicos on white top with plain back. Front brought to back as edge treatment. 88" square with 10 stitches per inch. / Collection of the Hess family.

Lydia Renninger Tyson b. 1839 d. 1868 Green Burr, Clinton County. / Appliquéd solid colored fabrics on white top with plain back. Applied solid colored binding. 81"×82" with 7-8 stitches per inch. / Collection of Mrs. S. B. Hardy.

Quilt by Margaret Louisa Witmer Smith b. 1832 Aaronsburg, Centre County, d. May 1926 Centre Hall, Centre County. / Appliquéd calico on white top with plain back. Applied calico binding. 88"×87" with 10 stitches per inch. / Collection of Elizabeth Smith Vonada.

Reedsville, Mifflin County. / Appliquéd calico on white top with plain back. Applied white binding. 89"×88" with 8 stitches per inch. / Private collection.

Many area appliqués were paper cut-out designs, like these. Most were from Union County but examples from Lycoming, Centre, and Mifflin counties attest to the fact that it was not an isolated phenomenon. Both of these also have superb needlework. The Centre County piece is quilted in rows as close as ¹/₄" apart which the Mifflin County example is ³/₈" apart. Margaret Louisa Witmer and her sister Anna Maria Witmer Wolfe b. 1928, made identical quilts probably pieced before Anna's marriage in 1854, of which this pink and white appliqué is one.

Margaret Louisa Witmer Smith in 1925 with her son Henry Witmer Smith and her granddaughter Elizabeth Smith. Courtesy: Elizabeth Smith Vonada.

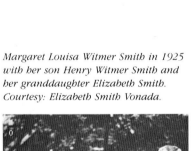

Quilt top by Esther Van Dyke b. circa 1830 Nippenose Valley, Lycoming County. / Pieced and appliquêd calico fabrics on white top, dated "1850." 70"×92" / Collection of Shirley A. Bierly

This top and an identical quilt were brought into the Williamsport documentation day by area families who had never met. The pieces were done by sisters of the Van Dyke family of the Nippenose Valley. The initials of the twelve siblings are sewn in red counted cross stitch in the center of each appliquêd patch. The quilt has been washed and lost some of its color but the top is like new and illustrates two period red calicos and three green ones. Counted cross stitch has been done on only one other area appliqué but paper cut-out designs are not uncommon. The cross stitch in the blocks reads from left to right and top row to bottom: "S/VAN/DYKE." "H/VAN/DYKE," "C/VAN/DYKE," "LJ/VAN/DYKE," "ESTHER/VAN DYKE M 26 1850," "JH/VAN/DYKE," "J·C·E/VAND/YKE," "JCJE/VAN/DYKE," "M/VAN DYKE," "S.M. KAUF/MAN," (for the oldest sister Margaret who had married a Kaufman), "EL/VAN/DYKE," and "WT/VAN/DYKE."

What little girl does not recollect her first piece of patchwork, the anxiety for fear the pieces would not fit, the eager care with which each stitch was taken, and the delight of finding the bright squares successfully blended into the pretty pattern. Another square and another, and the work begins to look as if in time it might become a quilt; then, as the little girl grows up to young ladyhood, the blushes flit across her cheek when, as she bends over her sewing, grandmamma suggests that making patchwork is a sign of matrimonial anticipations; then the mother, exercising all her ingenuity to make a pretty quilt for the little occupant of the cradle, until we go forward to the old grandmother, who finds patchwork the finest work her aged èyes and trembling fingers will permit her to undertake. From the house of the rich mother who finds expensive silk sewed in pretty patterns, the choicest covering for her darling, to the poor hovel, where every rag is treasured to eke out the winter quilt for the little ones, we find patchwork. Stories by famous authoresses, and patterns even by artists, are to be found on the subject of patchwork.

The greatest neatness and regularity are requisite in the arrangement of the pieces to form a patchwork pattern, and great taste may be displayed in the blending of the colors. There is, in this State, an institution for the reformation of girls who have been impressed for some crime; they are taught to sew neatly, and each one is allowed to exercise her taste and ingenuity in the manufacture of a patchwork quilt, which she is allowed to take away with her when she leaves. I have seen one hundred and fifty beds in this institution each covered with a different pattern of patchwork quilt; some were very tasteful and pretty, others not.

In an economical point of view there is great saving in patchwork quilts, if they are made from pieces of cloth already in the house which are useless for anything else; but if as I once knew a lady to do, you buy the finest, highest priced French chintz to cut up into inch pieces, it is not perhaps so great a saving as it would be to buy the quilt outright.

An old lady, an aunt of mine, one of the single sisterhood, is constantly making the most beautiful patchwork quilts. She has one made entirely of pieces of dresses worn by the different members of the family: this is her family quilt, and it really seems odd to see so many familiar pieces made into one article.

"Patchwork" by Ellen Lindsay / *Godey's Lady's Book* / February 1857 / p. 166

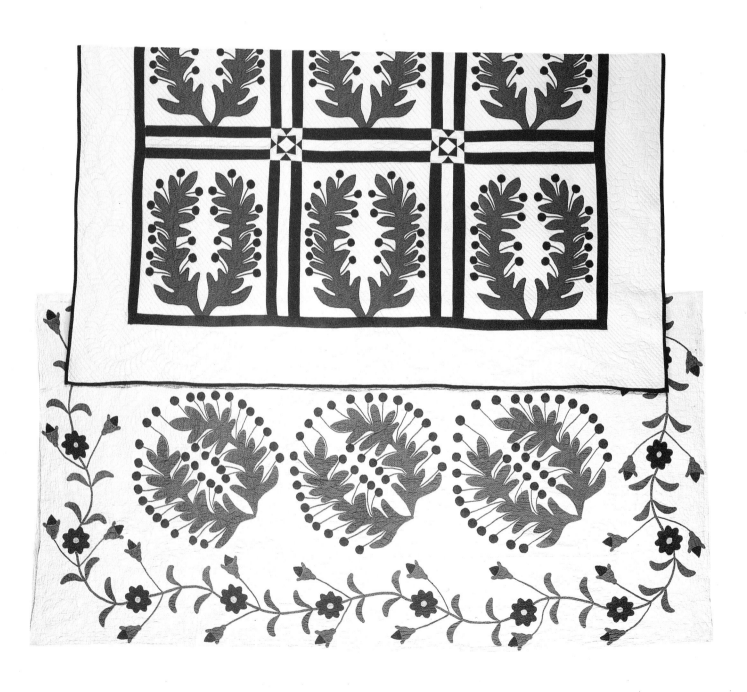

Quilt by Viola Susan Beahm Boyer b. 1875 d. 1947 Haines Township, Centre County and Eva Boyer Rearick b. 1914 Haines Township, Centre County. / Pieced and appliquéd solid colored and calico fabrics on white top with plain back. Applied solid colored binding. 84¹/₂"×77¹/₂" with 9-13 stitches per inch. / Collection by Eva L. Rearick.

Quilt by Dorcas Stine Rhodes b. 1838 Warrior's Mark, Centre County d. 1889 Oliver Township, Centre County. / Appliquéd solid colored and calico fabrics with some padded work on a white top with plain back. Front turned to back for edge treatment. 87¹/₂"×86" with 7-9 stitches per inch. / Private collection.

This quilt design was not seen until the final documentation day held in Lewistown, Mifflin County, when both quilts turned up within minutes of each other. The design source is not known. The one was made prior to 1889 and the other in 1930. The cherry stems are handled differently: the Rhodes piece uses a very thin appliquéd piece and the Boyer piece uses applied cording. The mother and daughter team made several fine twentieth century quilts; the husband, Newton William Boyer, making the marking patterns for them. The daughter credits her quilting experience and expertise to both her parents: her mother for attention to needlework detail and her father for design sense.

Quilt by Tama Boob Thompson b. 1891 Pleasant Grove, Union County d. 1984 Loganton, Clinton County. / Pieced and appliquéd solid colored fabrics on white top with plain back. Applied solid colored binding. 88"×89" with 10 stitches per inch. / Private collection.

Tama Boob Thompson was the third and last generation in a family of avid quiltmakers. Quilts of both her grandmothers and her mother as well a body of her own work were kept together. This quilt was done in the 1930s from a pattern Tama found in the Grit *and exhibits unusually fine and abundant stitching for a quilt of that era. The pencil marks on this quilt, like many found in area blanket chests, are still evident.*

See, everybody made their own dresses and they were scraps, leftovers from making that dress. And then they would exchange with the neighbors. You'd give them some of yours and they'd give some of theirs. That way you'd get a big variety of different designs.
Tama Thompson interview / May 29, 1974

We'd usually sit, mother and I, at night and quilt pretty late at night with the old oil lamp across the board. It's a wonder we have eyes today because you had to strain your eyes to see.
Tama Thompson interview / May 29, 1974

Never use lead pencils in marking a quilt, as in quilting the thread carrying back and forth through the pencil marks transfers the lead through to the cotton; many washings are necessary to remove lead marks.
Sears Century of Progress in Quilt Making / 1934 / p. 7

Sunbury area, Northumberland County./ Pieced and appliquéd solid colored fabrics on white top with plain back. Applied solid colored binding. 39"×34" with 9-10 stitches per inch. Collection of Verna B. Bzdil.

Sunbury area, Northumberland County. / Pieced and appliquéd calicos on white top with plain back. 51½"×48½" with 7-9 stitches per inch. Applied print binding. / Collection of Shirley and Robert Kuster.

The larger of the two crib quilts is nearly identical in the rendition of its cockscomb to full-sized examples of this pattern found across the Susquehanna River in Snyder County. The smaller example, the childhood crib quilt of Mrs. Fred Weaver of Sunbury, who was in her eighties when she died in 1943, is a more individualist approach to the same design.

Freeburg, Snyder County. / Pieced and appliquéd calico fabrics on white top with plain back. Applied calico binding. 84½" square with 7-8 stitches per inch. / Collection of Carol and Jim Bohn.

This Cockscomb appliqué is nearly identical to another from the Port Trevorton area of Snyder County. Both have reverse appliqué but this one has yet a fourth color—a pink calico. The saw tooth borders are unusual in that they are long strips of applied fabric rather than the fairly common pieced strips. This is a typical area mid-nineteenth century appliqué in its overall organization, palette, fabric types, and quilting designs.

Clara Drumheller taken by Schindlers, Sunbury. Courtesy: Mary Moll.

Shoemaker family quilt, West Buffalo Township, Union County. / Pieced calico fabrics with apron gingham back. Applied calico binding. 81"×75" with 6-8 stitches per inch. / Private collection.

Like many area quilts, the blocks are set on their points and touch their neighboring blocks, thereby forming continuous visual movement on the quilt's top. This has been found by Suellen Meyer in her study of Missouri's German quilts (Uncoverings, 1985) *to be a design preference there as well. The circular quilting in the fill-in blocks add interest to the quilt and their curved lines are picked up by the ocean wave quilting of the borders. These curves are juxtaposed by the quiltmaker to the hard edge of the piecing, thus making a simple quilt more complex and extremely pleasing visually. The thickness of the batting accentuates the overall effect. There are four different pink calicos and a single green calico in this pattern, sometimes called* Hovering Hawks *and probably made circa 1880-1920, a period of time in which the bulk of the area's extant quilts were done.*

Quilts by Clara Leitzel Drumheller b. 1883 d. 1939 Snyder County. / Pieced calico fabrics with apron gingham back. Applied calico binding. 86"×78" and 81½"×78" with 6-8 stitches per inch. / Collection of Mary Moll.

Sarah Stahl Snyder b. 1889 d. 1968 Buffalo Township, Union County. Pieced calico fabrics with print back. Applied calico binding. 79"×78" with 6 stitches per inch. Private collection.

Katherine Smith Seebold b. 1865 Limestone Township, Union County d. 1943 Troxelville, Snyder County Pieced calico and solid colored fabrics with apron gingham back. Applied calico binding. 76" square with 9 stitches per inch. Collection of Clarence Seebold.

These quilts' dominant palette is occasionally relieved by the use of a third or fourth color, albeit an usual one at times. Sarah Snyder's Brown Goose *was a pattern seen just once while Clara Drumheller's* Ocean Wave *was a fairly popular one in this area of Pennsylvania but her* Temperance Tree *is one that was not pieced here often. On the other hand, Katherine Seebold's* Basket with Fruit *(detail) was done in many variations, great number, and on vastly different scales. Twenty-three examples with applied handles were seen while thirteen were similar to Katherine's. The scale of the baskets went from 4½" to 13" across the top with the size of the pieced triangles varying accordingly.*

Katherine Smith Seebold on her wedding day in 1892. Courtesy: Clarence Seebold.

*Quilt by Lucinda White b. 1813 d. 1894
Lamar, Clinton County. / Pieced print
and solid colored fabrics on white top
with plain back. Applied print binding.
96″×83″ with 8-9 stitiches per inch. /
Collection of Isabel Hayes Packer.*

*The most delicate sawtooth border seen,
made of triangels ⅝″ long, frames
three edges of this large quilt, creating
a definite top, bottom, and sides. Most
area quilts do not have a distinct
top and bottom created by border
treatment or the placement the motifs
within the quilt. This piece is also
unusual in that the quilter used dark
thread to quilt the green areas and
white thread for the remainder. This
occurred on only a handful of pieces.
The pattern,* The Broken Star *or*
Carpenter's Wheel, *is one of the more
complex star patterns seen and the
palette, although it is in pinks and
greens, is not the usual small figured
calicos.*

Quilt by Margaret Brouse Ulrich b. 1854 d. 1926 Jackson Township, Snyder County. / Pieced calico fabrics on white top with plain back. Applied print binding. 91½"×82" with 8-9 stitches per inch. / Williams' collection.

The pieced fabrics here illustrate the judicious use of the typical pink and green calico palette, with the additional yellow, as well as superb quality quilting—fine, even, and abundant—done in double rows and various size princess feather wreaths.

Snyder County. / Pieced calicos with plain back. Applied calico binding. 38"×33" with 6-7 stitches per inch. / Collection of Shirley and Robert Kuster.

Pink and green calicos are placed alongside a red/rust one in this area crib quilt. Like some of the darker quilts, it is quilted in a colored thread. The inner sawtooth border is commonly used in area quilts to enclose the central overall block design as in this example.

Caroline Gutelius Shriner. Courtesy: Mary Maher.

Quilt, top, and patch by Caroline Gutelius Shriner b. 1828 d. 1898 Mifflinburg, Union County. / Pieced calicos, one with print back and applied calico binding. Quilt is 38"×29" with 8 stitches per inch; top is 42"×40"; patch is 23½" across. / Private collection.

Caroline Gutelius made a number of quilt tops before her marriage in 1846 and on one, made of feathered stars just like this patch, she signed her maiden name. Of her two crib quilt tops, one was quilted while the other with identical calico fabric remains as she left it. They are placed here with a Union County round oak sewing basket, 7"w.x9½"l.x6"h. with 3/16" rods, such as she might have used to hold her threads, needles, and pieces.

This is old-fashioned too; and I must allow it is very silly to tear up large pieces of cloth, for the sake of sewing them together again. But little girls often have a great many small bits of cloth, and large remnants of time, which they don't know what to do with; and I think it is better for them to make cradle-quilts for their dolls, or their baby brothers, than to be standing round, wishing they had something to do. The pieces are arranged in a great variety of forms: squares, diamonds, stars, blocks, octagon pieces placed in circles, &c. A little girl should examine whatever kind she wishes to imitate, and cut a paper pattern, with great care and exactness.

The Girl's Own Book, by Eliza Leslie / p. 225

Little girls often find amusement in making patch-work quilts for the beds of their dolls, and some even go so far as to make cradle-quilts for their infant brothers and sisters.

Patch-work may be made in various forms, as stars, triangles, diamonds, waves, stripes, squares, &c. The outside border should be four long strips of calico, all of the same sort and not cut into patches. The dark and light calico should always be properly contrasted in arranging patch-work.

Children may learn to make patch-work by beginning with kettle-holders, and iron-holders; and for these purposes the smallest pieces of calico may be used. These holders should be lined with thick white muslin, and bound all round with tape; at one corner there should be a loop by which to hang them up. Blower-holders are very convenient for the use of servants, to save their hands from scorching when they remove the blower from the coal-grate.

American Girl's Book, by Eliza Leslie / 1879 / pp.313-315

"Why such a puzzled look 'Mamsey'?" said Kate as we gathered around the evening lamp, for it was the "mail hour" in the country.

"I will refer you to Grandma," mother answered with a peculiar twinkle in her eyes.

Grandma adjusted her spectacles, read the miniature pink missive and informed us that "Mrs. Lenox has invited the ladies of this household to a quilting on next Thursday."

I read in the Resume of Fashion that the old time quilting bee is having a revival, and is now of marked importance to the average woman.

After considerable vacillation grandma consented to go to Mrs. Lenox's quilting. She enjoined each one "to be sure to take a thimble and threadcutter, a pair of scissors or a pocket knife."

"Well," said grandma, as Mrs. Lenox met her at the door, "forty years ago coming October I was here at a quilting, and I can think of but three of those that were here that day who are yet living. Outside of these sad recollections it is a rare pleasure to attend another quilting in this house, but I suppose I'll not be of much account?"

"Oh don't say that, for we need some one to lay off 'double diamonds'."

Grandma thought a spell, then took the pencil and ruler and marked the pattern as readily as if it were an everyday occurrence, and explained: They are just the same as single diamonds except you put two lines instead of one, say two parallel lines one-fourth inch apart, with a space one inch between each pair of lines to be crossed at right angles with similar spaced lines. This will give diamonds one-fourth inch and one inch square respectively, with divided spaces one inch long by one-fourth inch wide.

When twelve inches were quilted grandma declared it was time "to roll," saying that no one can reach farther than twelve inches and do good work on a quilt.

We all knew how to roll a quilt from the two opposite sides, but no one present, except grandma, knew how to roll it from all sides.

She ripped the quilt from the frames about two feet either side of each corner, which caused a triangular piece to hang at each corner. This was laid smoothly against the lining of the quilt, the frames loosened at each corner and all sides of the quilt rolled simultaneously, turning the frames downward, which brought the top side of the quilt on the top side of the roll.

The frames were again fastened securely and another depth of twelve inches quilted, when the quilt was unrolled and ripped two feet farther at either side of the corners and rolled as before. This method of rolling will allow more quilters to work than when rolled only from the two sides.

One question arose in regard to disposing of knots and fastening the ends of thread.

Grandma was appealed to decide this also.

"There are two ways," she informed us, "of hiding the knots. Some draw them through the lining, but I was taught not to put the right hand under the quilt. My method is to take a long stitch through the top of the quilt only, starting about an inch from where I wish to begin quilting, bringing the needle through where I wish the first stitch. Place the index finger of the left hand firmly when the needle was drawn through and pull the knot between the lining and and the top of the quilt."

"To fasten the ends of the threads take two or three back-stitches and clip it off, or take a long stitch, the same as in hiding the knot, and clip the thread."

"The latter plan is considered better, since the threads will not break so easily when washing the quilt."

"A Quilting Bee," by Fanny Love / *The National Stockman and Farmer* / April 23, 1896 / p. 16

The most serviceable of patchwork quilts are made from patches of calico joined together neatly, lined with white cotton, and made up with an interlining of sheet wadding, quilted in diamonds and bound with a bias strip of white or colored muslin. These quilts are easily made, easily laundered, and will last almost a lifetime.

There is no reason why the designs given on this page should not be utilized for silk patchwork quilts by those women who are fortunate enough to have silk patches, as well as the time required to put them together. The silk quilt is made up in exactly the same way as the cotton one, but as it may not be sent to the laundry neither the patches nor the lining selected should be very light in color.

The time was when patchwork quilts were seen only in farmhouses, where they were brought out when extra bed-covering was required, and, redolent of sweet lavender, formed the most comfortable and satisfactory of bed-coverings. But recently the city housekeeper has discovered how much more easily kept in order than either blanket or comforter is the patchwork quilt, which repeated visits to the laundry neither thickens nor fades, and she has made up her mind to add a few of these serviceable articles to her stock of winter bedcoverings. For her, as well as for the woman in the country, to whom the making of pachwork for quilts represents many pleasant moments, this page has been prepared.

"Twelve Designs for Patchwork Quilts," by Emma Elwell / *Ladies' Home Journal* / November 1896 / p. 24

The pieced cotton quilt, which has not been a possible bed-covering within the memory of the woman of to-day, has now become a most modish dressing for beds. The reappearance of the furniture of our forebears has quite naturally brought about a rehabilitation of the long-despised coverlets with which bridal chests were once so well plenished, and the modern housewife, casting a keen glance quiltward, has discovered that nothing, save perhaps the old hand-woven bedspread, so effectively drapes a mahogany four-poster as one of these gay quilts. She has also seen them used with effect upon brass, iron, or even modern wooden beds.

"A Thing 'of Shreds and Patches'," by Helen Blair / *The Ladies' Home Journal* / April 1902 / p. 53

The days of quilting, save at church sewing societies, are well-nigh over, though the cotton quilt of our grandmothers is in very good form, provided one has luckily been inherited.

"Household Hints," by Judith Gould / *House Beautiful* / February 1903 / p. 146

When the season of active church work was about to open, one of the societies in our guild sent out invitations to all the women of the parish to come to a rag-bag social, on a certain afternoon. The admission was a bundle of pieces of new material of any sort or description. A goodly store of remnants was received; cretonne, linen, silk, cotton, lace, bits of ribbon, odd skeins and spools of silk, all those things that every housekeeper puts away carefully thinking she will surely "need sometime," and usually doesn't. A committee of eight was appointed to look over—measure and classify the mass of material and plan articles into which it might be converted at our weekly meetings. It was surprising how the things fitted in; your piece and my piece together would make a useful article, which neither could have done alone.

Good Housekeeping / November 1907

There are many things to induce women to piece quilts. The desire for a handsome bed furnishing, or the wish to make a gift of one to a dear friend, have inspired some women to make quilts. With others, quilt making is a recreation, a diversion, a means of occupying restless fingers. However, the real inducement is love of the work; because the desire to make a quilt exceeds all other desires. In such a case it is worked on persistently, laid aside reluctantly, and taken up each time with renewed interest and pleasure. It is this intense interest in the work which produces the most beautiful quilts. On quilts that are made because of the genuine interest in the work, the most painstaking efforts are put forth; the passing of time is not considered; and the belief of the majority of such quilt makers, though unconfessed, doubtless, is the equivalent of the old Arab proverb that 'Slowness comes from God, but hurry from the devil.'

Quilts / Their Story & How to Make Them, by Marie Webster / 1926 / p. 155

Quilt by Margaret E. Frazier Vonada b. 1871 Salona, Clinton County d. 1960, Mackeyville, Clinton County. / Pieced print and solid colored fabrics with plain back. Applied solid colored binding. 77″×74″ with 6 stitches per inch. / Collection of Shirley Fox Hunt.

Around the World *quilts or those with a smaller series built around the same piecing techniques, often called* Philadelphia Pavement, *were done in some number here. They date from the third quarter of the nineteenth century through the Depression as seen here in Margaret Vonada's example which was pieced in 1937-1938 and quilted in the winter of 1940 with the help of her grand-niece, Mildred Walizer Fox. Its 6,887 pieces measure ³/₄″ square each.*

Margaret E. Frazier Vonada with Shirley Fox in 1949. Courtesy: Mildred Fox.

Quilt by Carrie Wolfe Aucker b. 1876 d. 1957 Union Township, Snyder County. / Pieced calico on white top with plain back. Applied calico binding. 37″×29¹/₂″ with 8 stitches per inch. / Collection of Edna May Aucker.

The blue and white quilts such as this crib quilt were usually made with a figured blue material—small white crescents, stars, circles, crosses—fabrics that had appeal over a long period of time but which were not used in a great number of quilts here alone or in combination with other colors.

Mifflinburg, Union County Pieced calicos on white top with plain back. Applied white binding. 88″×79″ with 11 stitches per inch. Collection of Jane Town Watson.

Quilt by Elizabeth Knauss Reish b. 1828 d. 1909 Mifflinburg, Union County. / Pieced calicos with print back. Front brought over to back as edge treatment. 79″×78″ with 6-8 stitches per inch. / Collection of Helen Ruhl Kerstetter.

These quilts illustrate the blue and the blue and white palette that was moderately popular here. The Drunkards Path *like other overall patterns such as the* Irish Chain, Wild Goose Chase, *and* Ocean Waves *was a favorite pieced pattern with twenty examples seen all dating from the 1870-1920 period. The* Delectable Mountains *was not seen nearly as often but was always executed in one print fabric against a white background creating a light, simple and clean appearance as seen here.*

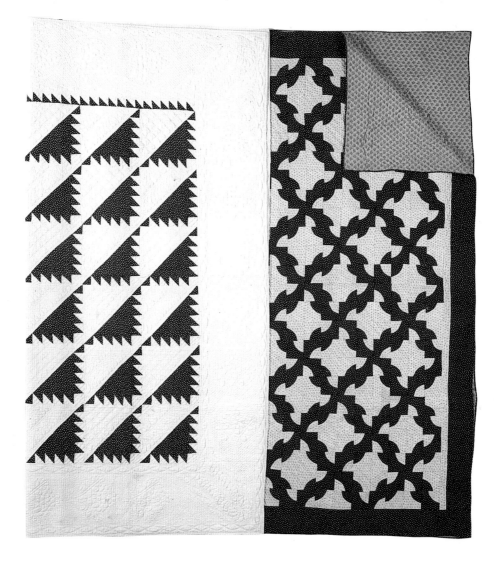

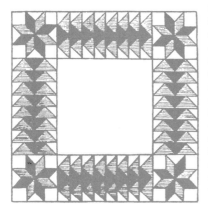

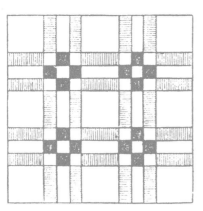

The vagaries of fashion are unaccountable and no one can tell in what direction they will lead next. Of late months everything which could be recognized as old-fashioned is the new fashion, and this is as truly the case in needlework as in sleeves or furniture. The decree has gone forth that a revival of patchwork quilts is at hand, and dainty fingers whose owners have known only patches and patchwork from family description are busy placing the blocks together in new and artistic patterns, as well as in the real old-time order.

In past days the artistic instinct that knew of no other outlet pleased itself often over intricate mosaics of calico, and we cannot despise the love of beauty that tried to express itself by form and color in simple material, though sometimes the time and labor bestowed seem to us to be altogether disproportionate to their object.

SOME OLD DESIGNS

The subjoined patterns are chosen with an effort to avoid the rock of ugliness and the whirlpool of intricacy. The design in Illustration No. 1 is taken from a quilt made nearly fifty years ago; it was called the Odd Fellows' March for some unknown reason, such as has prompted the naming of classic patterns, like the Irish Chain or Fox and Geese. The completed square measures sixteen inches; it was made of a finely flowered red print and white cotton. The squares were put together with strips of white about three inches wide.

For this pattern and others take a square of stiff paper the size of the square desired; rule it according to the diagram given; cut the several squares or angles required out of this diagram; add small seams when cutting the cotton, and the result will be an accurate and altogether satisfactory copy.

QUILT OF RED AND WHITE

No. 2 is a modification of the first. The square should be smaller and three shades of print could be used. The patch in Illustration No. 3 comes from a manse whose mistress says she has made four like this, finding the work covnenient while chatting with the frequent visitors incident to her position. The materials are Turkey red and white cotton. The centre square is ten and one-half inches, the surrounding strip is two inches wide. It is, perhaps, the most easily made and effective pattern that can be given. The quilt is made oblong by adding a strip at top and bottom, and can be made larger or smaller by altering the size of the centre square. Great care must, of course, be taken that all the patches are cut evenly and well.

A CRADLE QUILT

The design in Illustration No. 4 is a cradle quilt, made by a grandmother a good many years ago; the baby is now a stalwart man, but the little quilt is gay and pretty enough still to begin a second career of usefulness. The inner square measures seven and one-half inches, the stripe is four inches wide. It is made of two contrasting colors. The triangles on the side are from squares of about an inch. The corner stars, like the centre of No. 5, are formed of eight diamonds. The pattern is obtained by folding a four-inch square of paper diagonally twice; from the long points cut a square, and a triangle from between the other two points of the star. One diamond, the square and triangle will give the needed patterns. Even the deft Canadian who gave this pattern owned that it was a great deal of work, but the fact that it was for the baby's bed was an ample justification in her eyes. On a larger scale the border might be used very effectively.

From the same source Illustration No. 5 was obtained. Nine of these stars, enclosed in a narrow border of diamonds, brightened the bed. Three shades of red print were used. I think this is one of the most aesthetic patterns of the olden time; still it may be new to many of the rising generation. I would not recommend any one to put nine stars on one quilt, but one star enlarged according to taste and eight bordered or not as preferred, would make a pretty centerpiece. By employing more shades the star can be enlarged, as well as by increasing the size of the diamond used in the centre. A smaller star in silk could be used for a cushion, and making it would form a pleasant task for fingers unskilled in embroidery.

TWO SIMPLE PATTERNS

Illustrations No. 6 and No. 7 will atone by their simplicity for the difficulty of the last pattern. The completed square of No. 6 measures nine inches. The squares are joined together, light to dark, so that four squares apparently form a larger square. The diagram is so simple that no directions are necessary, and the same may be said of No. 7. This has been known as the album quilt unfortunately, which may prejudice some against the neat little squares that look so pretty either in blue and white or pink and white. Both of these last are given for the sake of beginners, so they will not need much instruction or help. The circle of No. 5 before the rays of the star begin is sometimes set in a square of white, which is bordered with colored diamonds. This arrangement makes a very pretty quilt.

In following any of these designs it must not be forgotten that small pieces of any kind of colored print may be utilized. The general effect is not so good without uniformity, of course; but with care one may avoid unpleasing incongruities of color.

FINISHING THE QUILT

After having made the patchwork of the desired dimensions tack two layers of wadding on the inner side. Then make a lining of soft, white cotton exactly the same size, and baste it very carefully upon the wadded patchwork. Be lavish with your basting thread, running it around the edges diagonally from corner to corner, and across again, after the fashion of the Union Jack; give it some additional lines until the patchwork and lining are smoothly and firmly fastened together and ready for the final process of quilting.

The old-fashioned quilting bars, into which the work is now ready to be fastened, insure the most perfect results. The lines that are to be followed with a light-running stitch are marked with colored chalk in diamonds or squares of any angle or size preferred. A quilting bee is the merriest and quickest way of finishing the quilt after all preliminary preparations have been made. If the quilting bars and the bee are not attainable the work may be spread upon a bed, and with a little extra care and trouble may be quilted in that way. The worst way of all is to use the sewing machine for the purpose, and the best is to find some skillful, old-fashioned sewing woman who will take your dainty, bright patchwork, line it, quilt it in delicate, fine tracery, and bind it for as moderate a sum as the making of a print dress.

A well-made quilt will last in constant use for many years, and can be renovated by re-covering when worn or faded.

The old-fashioned art of patchwork can never become entirely obsolete while there are in the majority of households little fingers just learning to hold the needle, or failing eyes that require some simple occupation or pastime.

The result of the hours pleasantly spent over the bright-colored fragments is always acceptable to the good house mother, for these pieced quilts are light, warm, durable and easily cleansed.

All of these patterns may be varied or modified according to taste, but a fixed principle should be to make white the basis of all, and to use only solid colors or a tiny-patterned bright print as the contrast. If this is done the inner patchwork quilt will always be a pretty as well as a useful part of the bed covering. In many respects it is preferable to the cumbrous puff which has displaced it of late years.

"Revival of the Patchwork Quilt," by Sybil Lanigan / *The Ladies' Home Journal* / October 1894 / p. 19

When the patchwork was completed it was laid on the lining with layers of wool or cotton wadding between, and the edges were basted all around. It was then ready for the quilting frame. Many of these old-time bedspreads dispensed with the patchwork and were merely quilted. These were termed "pressed quilts" and were very often made in white and cream washing materials. They were often finished off with hand-made netted fringes, a work of art in themselves. Most intricate designs were employed in the making of these pressed quilts, and sometimes not a quarter of an inch of surface would be without quilting stitches.

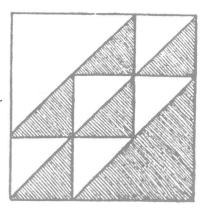

The Ladies' Home Journal, *October 1894*

In the earlier days a very laborious process of marking was resorted to. A string was dipped in thick starch and then was placed on the quilt and tapped so that the mark of the starch was impressed on the quilt. This left a faint line, that could be brushed off when the quilting was done. Later, different-colored chalks were used. These days of ready-marked materials for needlework and of practical methods of transferring patterns make us realize that the old-time methods must have been very tiresome.

When a counterpane has been quilted, it needs finishing neatly. There are several ways of doing this. The piece is taken out of the frame and laid on a large table and cut evenly on the four sides. The edges are turned in and seamed or bound in white, or, if it is a silk courre-pied, it is done with a pretty colored ribbon that harmonizes with the predominating shades. Sometimes when the quilt consists of a set pattern done in one solid color on a light ground, two or three inches of the dark shade is used for the border.

All kinds of fancy stitches were used to embellish the quilts—herring-bone, outline stitch and cross stitch. Sometimes a dainty little flower was worked in embroidery silk in each pattern, and again accent was given by a spot of dark color worked in silk. Occasionally a bold flower was outlined to bring it into strong relief. In fact, there was no end to the ideas and contrivances for making this handicraft original and distinctive.

In looking at old-time patchwork quilts, the day in which they were made can be told by the prints and calicoes that were used in their make-up. The old-time prints were certainly much more beautiful than those of to-day, but in the earlier Colonial days calicoes were scarce, and old woolen garments and worn-out flannel sheets and old coat linings were brought into service, after first being dipped in the family dyepot of old-blue or madder.

Long ago bits of stuff were sold in small bundles at country auction, and many were the keen bidders who bought up these remnants, which were usually woolen. Quilts made of washing materials were a later innovation.

It is like listening to a story to hear some old lady tell of "my daughter's wedding-gown" or "my son's cloak," all of which were worked into her beautiful old quilts.

"Old Time Quilting," by Mable Tuke Priestman / *The Designer* / October, 1910 / p. 372

Quilt by Christena Pontius b. 1785 d. 1877 Mifflinburg, Union County. / Pieced chintz and calicos with plain back. Back turned to front as an edge treatment. 92"×90" with 6-7 stitches per inch. / Collection of Ruth Zimmerman.

In a note attached to this quilt, signed in 1903 by Mary Anne Catherine Pontius Gemberling, herself a quilter, she identifies the work as being done by her mother, Christena Pontius. She noted that the dark calico in the star was dress scraps from Christena's mother and that Christena pieced the quilt so that she might remember her. Catherine (b. 1836, d. 1907) also noted that the thread was homemade. The back is quite coarse. The note emphasized that it "Not be sold out of the family."

Stahl family quilt, Buffalo Township, Union County. / Pieced chintz and calico fabrics with plain back. Back brought to front as edge treatment. 91¼"×90½" with 8-9 stitches per inch. / Private collection.

This is one of three pieced chintz quilts seen. It was thought by the family to have been made by one of two women in the late nineteenth century. Its coarse back, linen thread, and fabrics, primarily of three designs, push its date back to the late 1830s. Like the vast majority of area pieces, all aspects of this quilt were hand sewn. The sewing machine was not invented until approximately ten years later (1846), becoming a common household machine after the Civil War.

Quilt by Mary Magdelena Bibighaus Piper b. 1803 Northampton County d. 1876 Mifflinburg, Union County. / Pieced calico and solid colored fabrics on white top with plain back. Applied calico binding. 91"×89" with 8-9 stitches per inch. / Collection of Katherine Roush.

The single large pieced star, usually called Bethlehem Star, Blazing Star, or Lone Star by their owners, was, and still is, considered to be the tour de force of local pieced quilts. They are usually set off, as in this example, with a saw tooth, rickrack or band border. The white areas were often quilted with princess wreaths, with an undulating princess feather in the border. This star is one of the earlier examples of the type, having an oral tradition of being made in 1836. Over 104 different pieced star patterns have been counted.

Quilt by Nancy Elizabeth Hall Bitner b. 1844 d. 1922 Salona, Clinton County. / Pieced calicos on white top with plain back. Back brought to front for edge treatment. 83½" square with 8 stitches per inch. / Collection of Beatrice Miller. Photo: Bridget Allen.

128 diamond-shaped pieces, an inch long, make up each of the twenty-five small pieced stars of the Bitner quilt. Though washed frequently, the thoughtful color combinations and the myriad of quilting designs, demonstrate that this seamstress was in no hurry to get her work done. This is truly a quilter's quilt, one which they love to touch and discuss at length. It is sewn with a six-ply thread which was available here after 1840, imported at first from Scotland and made there by Coats or the Clark Brothers. Three-ply thread predates the six-ply.

A 'quilt' is a thing of beauty, broadly speaking; and on the same basis it is an artistic production. On the theory that 'Satan finds some mischief still, for idle hands to do,' it has doubtless proved a good deal of an anti-Satanic influence in the world. How many a callous 'lord of creation' has scoffed and laughed at his toiling wife, sister or daughter, for 'cutting cloth up into little bits of pieces for the sake of sewing them together again!' But the patient woman has toiled on, without rejoinder; for, was it not indispensable to her peace of mind that her 'blazing star of Mexico' should blaze more brilliantly than that of her neighbor, whose work was the admiration of the community of favored inspectors; or that her 'crazy patchwork' should be crazier than that of some one else?

Good Housekeeping / June 1894 / p. 263

The mother had cleared the dinner away,
    Her busy hands were free.
The boyish swarm was tired and warm;
    The mother—a thought thought she—
'They're tired of their toys, my dear little boys,
    I'll have a sewing-bee."

At her call came Willy and Walter
    With sweetly earnest air.
The sunshine, bright from the world of light
    Gleamed in their golden hair,
And fragrant showers from spicy showers
    Stole in to greet them there.

She fitted them each to a thimble,
    (Such tiny hands to sew!)
Through the needle's head she drew the thread;
    ('Twas forty years ago.)
And she showed the way most patiently
    To draw it to and fro.

"Carefully take each stitch," she said,
    "Even as even can be."
This way, that way, in and out, they
    Counted "one, two, three."
The baby bound by the droning sound,
    Fell asleep on her knee.

Together she basted the pieces,
    The somber and the gay,
From closet and press, from baby's dress,
    Yellow and green and grey.
And the mother smiled at her boys beguiled;
    For they thought 'twas only play.

Lovingly over the pretty work
    Their little fingers flew.
With stitches strong, though crooked and long,
    'twas done before they knew.
And with pride they told of their baby bold
    Who made one square of blue.

'Twas forty years ago, you know.
    Where can the children be?
The precious spread now covers my bed,
    For Willie married me.
And Walter small, is large and tall
    And he has babies three.

The other? Ah, he went to God
    While yet the quilt was new.
There's not one thread of the patchwork spread
    So tenderly we view,
As the baby's square in the corner there,
    That little square of blue.

"The Patchwork Spread," by Emily J. Langley /
Good Housekeeping / January 7, 1888 / p. 115

Our young ladies of the present generation know little of the mysteries of "Irish chain," "rising star," "block work," or "Job's trouble," and would be as likely to mistake a set of quilting frames for clothes poles as for anything else. It was different in our younger days.

"The Quilting Party," by T.S. Arthur / *Godey's Lady's Book* / August 1849 / p. 185

During our warm summer weather we had sewing classes, in which we taught our young girls how to sew and piece quilts. We found it one of the best ways of teaching our girls how to use a needle, and really an economical way too, for every household has more or less to spare, and the quilts are always salable. Plain nine square is one of the best patterns for very new beginners; after that the road to California and back, or the wedding knot, or the haystack. Any of these are pretty and easy to piece.

Start a sewing class or society. I do think there should be one in every community. It pays in a matter of economy, and pays parents to have their girls know how to sew. Now is a good time to commence one, before the long winter evenings. In these classes work is play, the girls become interested, compare their work, and quite naturally strive to excel. We have a nice variety of patterns in our class. If any one wants new patterns, send stamps to pay postage and I will send them to you. We have the road to California and back, king's crown, castle stairs, moon and stars, devil's puzzle, Ducthman's puzzle, old maid's puzzle (you see we favor puzzles) and robbing Peter to pay Paul, pin-cushion and cucumbers, Centennial, bear's paw, wheel of fortune, wedding knot, mother's fancy, hit and miss,—this uses pieces of all sorts and sizes,—also haystack, button string, toad in a puddle, Texas tears, Texas star, coffin star, maple leaf, box, Garfield's monument. This is a lovely pattern; the letter G in the center of the white monument, and that set on a dark ground makes a very pretty quilt. Then we also have the ocean wave, basket, northern star, sweet gum leaf, brick wall, broken dishes, double T, blind man's fancy, hearts and gizzards, monkey wrench, tangled garter, and sunflower; this last one makes quite a showy spread. You can send a stamp for postage on any one of these patterns, or send ten or a dozen stamps and I will send you by mail all the patterns I have mentioned, and if you wish I will make and send you a paper block with each pattern, so you can see just how they look before commencing one of them. I will also give directions what colors to use, etc., where necessary.

By Mrs. F.A.W., East Saginaw, Mich. / *Good Housekeeping* / October 26, 1889 / p. 311

In the present extensive course of girls' study, when little tots of tender years are expected to surpass in learning all that their grandmother knew in her teens, and the "girl graduate" displays the blue-ribboned diploma crediting her with knowledge of the 'ologies which her grandmother could scarcely have pronounced, there is one branch of industry which can receive but little attention. The home needle, which gave the women of earlier generations employment and amusement, has lost its former importance; the machine has usurped its place, and so cheapened work that the busy housewife says with truth, 'It is cheaper to buy than to make.' In the constantly widening field of women's work, the home needle can never be expected to resume its former place.

Good Housekeeping / September 1896 / p. 105

Will someone kindly tell through these columns how to piece an old-fashioned blazing star quilt, such as our grandmothers used to piece years ago, and oblige a farmer's wife?

"The Blazing Star Wanted," by Mrs. Albert Colcord / *The National Stockman and Farmer* / April 21, 1898 / p. 18

We have viewed the family portraits o'er and rummaged the garret thro,'
And we've eaten the finest country meal Grandmother could bake and brew,
And our cup of contentment is brimming up, it actually seems 'tis spilt,
As we lay to rest in the four-post bed, under the Patchwork Quilt.

The Patchwork Quilt, dear Grandmother says, that is covering you and me,
Is the very same quilt made long ago, one night at the Quilting Bee;
Gay with diamonds, circles and squares of yellow and green and red,
The neighbors collected from far and near to fashion it, 'twas said.

Cookies and cider were handed about, when they gathered in the barn,
And the lassies' dainty fingers flew, while the lads told many a yarn;
Then the Patchwork Quilt was folded up and carefully laid away,
To be shaken free from its lavender sprigs on Dorcas' wedding day.

Now Dorcas's Dorcas will tuck us in, with a loving good night kiss,
And if she speaks of the Patchwork Quilt, she'll be apt to tell you this—
That if you shut your eyes up tight and tuck it around you so,
You are sure to dream of the Quilting Bee—in the beautiful long ago."

"The Patchwork Quilt," by Mary Small Wagner / *The Designer* / May 1904 / p. 69

Quilt by Catherine Albach Heiser m. circa 1840 d. 1892 Buffalo Township, Union County. / Pieced calico and solid colored fabrics with apron gingham back. Applied calico binding. 80¹/₂"×79¹/₂" with 7 stitches per inch. / Collection of Cherry Will.

Several dozen quilts from the Heiser and Jodon families were handed down for five generations in this early Union County family. Favorites were sometimes copied by succeeding generations. Often a single pattern was pieced or appliquêd for each grandchild of a particular generation. As one of the descendents, Sara Heiser Reigle, recalled in looking at all the quilts: "Well, the Heisers really could use color boldly, but the Jodons did much finer stitching." This star is from the earliest generation of Heisers whose work still exists. Catherine's solid figured background is unusual for this area.

Hubler family pillowcase, East Buffalo Township, Union County. / Pieced in calicos with plain back. 28¹/₂"×20¹/₂" / Collection of Mr. and Mrs. Robert Hubler.

Along with family-made comforts and quilts, this pillow case was stored in the family home that was built in 1850 in the center of Buffalo Valley. The family has lived in the area since 1793 and on the present farm for six generations. The pillow case was the most exceptional piece found in the attic by the present generation. Other pieced cases, though we suspect they were made here, have not been documented nor whimsies, pockets, chair pads or backs either, although they too might have been pieced by area women.

Sheary family quilt, Lewisburg, Union County. / Pieced calicos with plain back. Back brought to front as edge treatment. 85½" square with 8-9 stitches per inch. / Collection of Edna M. Sheary.

Quilt by Susan Jodon Heiser b. 1874 d. 1930 Buffalo Township, Union County. / Pieced calicos with apron gingham back. Front brought to back as edge treatment. 85¾"×83¼" with 7-8 stitches per inch. / Collection of Cherry Will.

Both of these Union County Variable Stars reflect the great number of examples seen (47). Next to the nine patch it was the favorite pieced pattern in the area. The Sheary family quilt exhibits the wide variety in rust-colored calicos available in the last quarter of the nineteenth century while the Heiser quilt uses two navy and white figured prints backed by the ubiquitous apron gingham. The quilts do not have the homemade applied bindings that most of the area quilts have and which were often made of contrasting fabric to set off the quilt but rather have the front brought around to the back and visa versa. Both were constructed of simple block designs. The Sheary quilt being more typical in that the blocks are set on point and touch each other thereby creating fill-in blocks of equal size. The Heiser quilt has its blocks set square and set apart by a sash or rake (called slip or garter elsewhere). Here, the sash becomes a prominent feature in the overall design. There are no small pieced patches within the sash to connect the blocks to each other, so the pieced star blocks float on a field of blue calico that acts like a starry night. The Heiser quilt was made between 1893-1900 while Susan Jodon was living at the Ruhl Farm. The last one she found time to quilt was in 1915 but she made quilt tops long after that. As her daughter, Sara Heiser Reigle recalled there was so much to do that her mother left the quilting of the tops go to another, less busy, day which never did arrive as farm and family responsibilities increased. In contrast, Susan's maiden sister, Flora, quilted continuously and was often seen sitting at her frame which was placed to catch the light, in front of the bay window of her Buffalo Crossroads home.

A quilt was oft'-times framed,
    Before the quilters came,
All neatly dressed in homespun goods,
In ruffled caps and quilted hoods
    Of antique name and fame.

They came with quaint work-baskets, and
    Still quainter reticules;
With snuff and thimbles, chalk, and wax,
With cut-and-dry in paper packs,
    Clay pipes and little stools.

The weather and health were first discussed,
    And then, at length, the news;
Next was the waning fire rebuilt,
And quilters seated 'round the quilt,
    Their forms and figures chose.

The various figures were laid off
    In chalk, or pencil-lines;
One worked an antique vase or jar,
Another worked as pretty a star
    As in the heavens shines.

Another worked "the Lover's Heart"—
    A broken one—who knows?
Another, still, a pretty fawn,
An eagle, pelican, or swan,
    White as the virgin snows.

I see them bending o'er their tasks,
    On every stitch intent;
Each striving hard to do her best
To rival and outdo the rest—
    On ne plus ultra bent. . . .

They munch the lusty ginger-cake
    and sip the currant wine;
Now cake and wine their tongues inspire—
Their conversation rises higher,
    And they begin to shine.

O, mocking wine! so dost thou oft'
    Content us with our lot;
While upturned spec's bestride the head
And cheeks and noses are turning red
    Life's troubles are forgot'.

Such conversation as that was
    No otherwhere was heard—
Where nine good talkers, for the nonce,
All spoke the same thing, all at once,
    And each the final word.

And, thus, revived and reassured,
    The work goes bravely on;
They laugh, they talk, they sneeze, they jest,
Still, each one tries to do her best
    And bravely holds her own.

How pleasant and how fair the sight,
    When women thus agree!
And how like homage paid to truth,
When Age thus dons the bloom of youth
    At three score years and—three.

And, still, the work goes bravely on—
    'Tis work a quilt adorns—
They little dream that 'neath that spread
Some conquer'd hero may lie dead,
    Or statesman may be born.

They know, indeed, it may adorn
    Some humble bridal-bed,
But little dream, that when they're gone
That faded patch-work quilt may form
    The shroud of "Union-dead," . . . .

Yet, still, the work goes bravely on—
    Work that the quilt adorns;
But now, of headache one complains,
Another of rheumatic pains,
    Another of her corns,

Which like old Probabilities,
    But "seldom ever" fail
To "indicate"—as goes the phrase—
The coming clear or rainy days,
    The snows, the frost and hail.

Says one, "just look at Mrs. Grove—
    Indeed, this woman's sick!
Get the camphor! she's goint to faint—
Hysterics! O, that mean complaint—
    Bring camphor! hartshorn! quick!"

Another wants the doctor "fetched"
    And thinks she should be bled;
Another calls for camomile—
"'Before the doctor comes three mile'
    This woman may be dead!"

"Just get her on the bed," says one,
    "And make some bitter tea—
Old man, old woman, homely things—
Open her cap and apron strings,—
    Now, let us wait and see!"

But, Mrs. Commonsense, at last
        Thus raised her voice and spoke—
"Let those who will, the tea prepare,
Just open the door and get fresh air—
        This air's enough to choke!"

The kitchen-door was opened, wide,
        And in the odors came—
Of coffee, ham-and-eggs and steaks,
Of sausage, biscuit, flannel-cakes,
        To cheer the fainting dame.

She raised her head, she smiled and said,
        "I want no bitter tea;
And never mind about fresh air—
A cup of good strong, coffee's air
        And tea enough for me." . . . .

And now the sumptuous table's spread,
        And all the guests sit 'round;
Now mother sits in father's place,
And gracefully she says a grace
        In silence most profound.

So, now, the savory feast proceeds
        And "good digestion waits
On appetite," while cheerful girls
With glowing cheeks and flowing curls
        Attend and help the plates. . . .

And so they sit and chat and sip
        And praise the rich repast;
Inquire how this and that was made—
How much for this and that was paid,.
How much of this and that it takes

To make such new-styled fancy cakes;
        And at the very last
Each one, just for a final sup,
Consents to take "just half a cup,"
But erring goodness fills it up.

(What real benefits we lose
        In more instead of less!
The golden mean no mischief works—
It's in the overflow, where lurks
        The siren of excess.)

Their cups were followed by their pipes—
        Their pipes by still more chat;
They talked of,—Heaven knows only what,
But I, alas, have now forgot'
        More than the half of that.

They talked of matrimonial things,
        And of elopements, more;
And most of all, the latest one—
That cunning one of farmer John
        And his belov'd Lenore.*

But, still, there was another thing—
        In this they were perplexed;
In gossip, 'though all posted well,
The newsiest one could not, just, tell
        Who would be married next.

But e'er the quilters separate
        The quilt must be complete;
So, each one, now, resumes her place
And quietly they quilt a race—
        No telling where they'll meet.

Methinks I hear, as then, I heard,
        The purring of the cat,
But did not hear a woman speak—
"The golden silence of the Greek"
        Now took the place of chat.

And when the handy work is done
        I know they won't decline—
That is to say, refuse to take
Just one more slice of that good cake.
        And one sm-a-ll glass of wine.

And when the noble task was done—
        Of labor, skill and love—
'Twas like a starry decoration,
Or some bright, glorious, constellation
        In that blue vault above.

Thus, were the finest bed-quilts made
        By hands,—at rest up there;
O, for the slumbers once enjoyed
Beneath such covers, unannoyed
        By trouble, pain, or care!

Time never wearies in his flight—
        His march no truce delays;
As quilts were made by thrifty wives,
So various are our checkered lives,
        And passing are our days—
As quilts, at firesides made and rolled,
Our lives like fireside tales are told.

"The Quilting," by H.L. Fisher / *Olden Times:
Or Pennsylvania Rural Life Some Fifty Years
Ago* / 1888 / pp. 145-154

As the old-time quilter of average proficiency could accomplish above five yards of plain quilting an hour, a thousand yards meant some 200 hours of work. In 1861 such work, at $2.00 a quilt, was worth a cent an hour.

Old Patchwork Quilts and the Women Who Made Them, by Ruth Findley / 1929 / p. 95

It is not quite fair to say that when we patch bedquilts we cut up the whole cloth into bits for the sake of sewing it together again, because the fact is, the cloth is already cut up and this is an ingenious way of using scraps. The greatest pitfall in the making of patchwork is that we are likely not to have scraps enough of two or three, or even half a dozen colors, so we are tempted to mix things horribly instead of combining them. It is perhaps not probable that we will have enough pieces from two or three summer gowns to make a whole bedquilt, and yet this is not unlikely either if we use white or a few yards of one solid color as a kind of keynote or setting to the harlequin combination. If you arrange bands of solid color systematically you may venture to mix little pieces in other bands. However, a thoughtful combination is always better than mixing.

"Some New Designs in Patchwork," by Mrs. Wilson / *The Ladies' Home Journal* / October 1907 / p. 90

As the time of the year is fast approaching for those happy in-door evenings with their pleasant and easy occupations which help to make home so dear, we think it requisite that we should offer a suggestion for one of those tasteful works which are of ceaseless variety in their execution, and are, when completed, worthy of becoming family heir-looms. The pattern supplied in our illustration is most effective. The contrast of color must, of course, be left to the taste of the worker, the only thing necessary to observe being the shade, the dark, the neutral, and the light, being all equally important for the general effect.

We intend to continue these patchwork patterns.

Godey's Lady's Book / January 1857 / p. 72

Folded up neatly by hands still for aye,
Just as she left them in bright array,
Rusty the needle the slim thread holds,
Now lying loosely among the pink folds;
Tears dim my eyes, I remember that day,
Then fold Grandma's patchwork and lay it away.

There are blocks there of pink and blocks of deep blue,
And all that is bright and cheery of hue,
For Grandma loved all that was cheerful and bright.
She loved the dear flowers and the warm morning light,
Though Grandma had sorrows we all of us knew,
And burdens to bear and they were not few.
How many the tears that were shed who can say
Over Grandma's dear patchwork safe folded away!
With always a thought for the dear ones at home,
And a smile for the lad who loved dearly to roam.

I can see her sweet face as she kneels by his side,
Blessing over and over her joy and her pride,
As she said in a voice so tender and cheery,
     "Don't worry, dear heart;
      'Twill not better your part,
Grandma's traveled a long, long way, deary!"

So when busied with cares of the household each day,
Often vexed with mere trifles, though light,
I look on those blocks of pink and they say,
"Darling, see! there is much that is bright!"
And there rings out again that voice so gay,
That voice so winning and cheery,
     "Don't worry, dear heart;
      'Twill not better your part,
Grandma's traveled a long, long way, deary!"

And with gladness I see in that one passing ray
The light and the brightness of by-gone day,
In Grandma's dear patchwork folded away.

"Grandma's Patchwork," by Mary Margaret Day / *Good Housekeeping* / April 26, 1890 / p. 298

Quilt by Elizabeth Gebhart Hoy b. 1829 d. 1864 Union County. / Pieced calicos on white top with plain back. Applied print binding. 89½″×81½″ with 8 stitches per inch. / Collection of Eleanor and Donald Hoy.

Stitches per inch alone do not reflect the quality of needlework as seen in this Union County example. The straightness and evenness of sewing as well as the nearness of rows and the complexity of patterns make it a particularly fine example, finer than some that have more stitches per inch. The sun or starburst patterns and another, called the Mariner's Compass, *were particularly challenging pieced designs and without exception they are area heirlooms that exhibit particularly fine quilting in the white areas. This tradition of exceedingly fine and abundant quilting in whole cloth areas comes from the quilting traditions of the British Isles where according to studies done in Devon, Somerset, Wiltshire, Durham, Cambria, Northumberland, and Wales such quilting was done as a home industry rather than as a craft or pastime as late as the third quarter of the nineteenth century. We see similar very fine quilting on pieces made here as late as 1875 but more frequently on earlier examples. Although quiltmaking was done in numerous countries over the centuries, it has been conceded that it evolved beyond a necessity to become an indigenous art form in design and needlework technique among African blacks, the Dutch, and the English, Welsh, and Scots.*

Quilt by Dora Mensch Musser b. 1865 d. 1953 West Buffalo Township, Union County or Sarah Stahl Snyder b. 1889 d. 1968 Buffalo Township, Union County. / Pieced calico and print fabrics with apron gingham back. Applied solid colored binding. 84"×82½" with 6-8 stitches per inch. / Private collection.

The organization of all of this family's quilts is superb and revolves, as in this example, around a series of seemingly small decisions regarding the choice of fabric back, binding, main and inner border colors and corner blocks, both small and large. It is apparent in viewing the total output of these women that they frequently purchased fabric specifically for their quilts. This is true of nearly all the area's appliqués and of a good proportion of the pieced quilts no matter how simple.

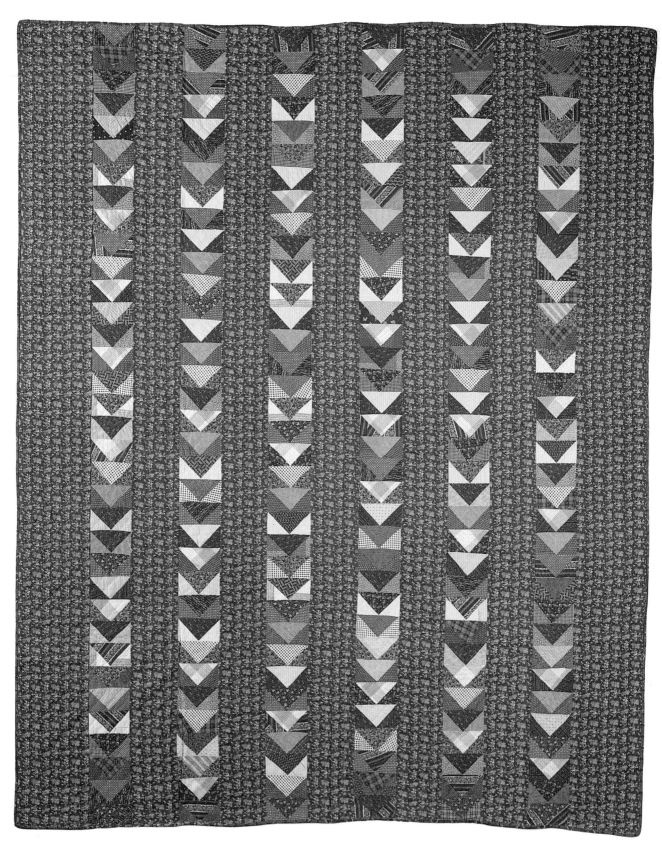

Quilt by Emma Gundy Kunkle b. 1854
d. 1945 East Buffalo Township, Union
County. / Pieced calico and print fabrics
with plain back. Applied print binding.
93½"×75½" with 6-8 stitches per inch.
/ Williams' collection.

This is a real scrap quilt offset by
the use of strong vertical panels of
purchased fabric. A number of the
green triangles were formed by several
related pieced calicos sewn together
in order to form a piece of the size
required.

Pennsdale, Lycoming County. / Pieced print and solid colored fabrics with plain back. Applied solid colored binding. 100"×88¾" with 10 stitches per inch. / Collection of the Packwood House Museum, Lewisburg.

Pennsdale, Lycoming County. / Pieced solid colored fabrics with print back. Front turned to back as edge treatment. 88"×86" with 6-8 stitches per inch. / Collection of the Lycoming County Historical Museum.

Both quilts exhibit the palette, fabric types, and attention to detail associated with Pennsylvania's Quaker quilts. The Court House Steps *quilt was part of the Kirk estate from Pennsdale, a fine collection of Quaker material given to the county historical society in 1979.* Log Cabin *types such as this were made mostly mid-nineteenth century. They were only moderately popular in this area and done either in all wools, cottons, or a combination of silks and velvets. The border and back of this piece are later than the top. The* Odd Fellows *pieced quilt is part of the Edith Fetherston collection which was purchased primarily in the local area and presumed to come from the single large Quaker community within it. Its back is a glazed chintz and its top of silks as in the Kirk piece. The Kirk estate also included quilted petticoats which Tandy Hersh pointed out in a paper* (Uncoverings, 1985) *might have as many as 17 stitches per inch.*

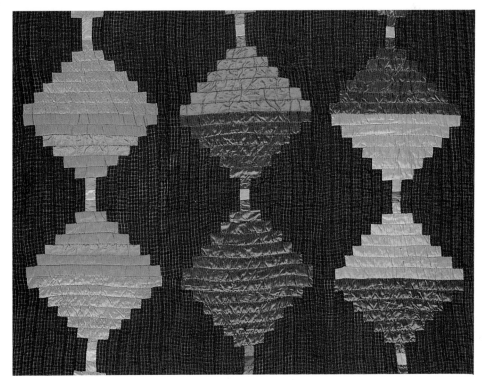

Hubler family hap, East Buffalo Township, Union County. / Pieced solid and print fabrics with plain back. Edges turned in and bound by blanket stitch in red thread. 72"×60½" with 5-6 stitches per inch. / Collection of Mr. and Mrs. Robert Hubler.

One of many area comforts, comfortables, or haps which were pieced designs of mixed fabric types that were filled with wool. Often they were quilted instead of knotted. By knotting or tying comforts, the owner was able to untie them, remove the wool, and clean the top and back when necessary, then reassemble the layers for continued use. This derives from the Germanic tradition of cleaning feather ticks.

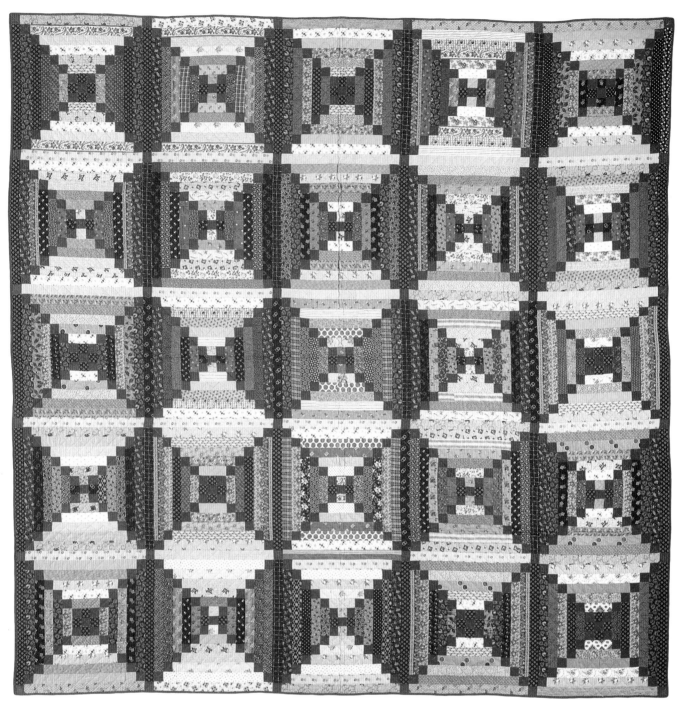

Sheary family quilt, Lewisburg, Union County. / Pieced calico and solid colored fabrics with apron gingham back. Applied solid colored binding. 79" square with 7-8 stitches per inch. / Collection of Edna M. Sheary.

The Court House Steps, *a pattern of light and dark fabrics that is consistently arranged as seen here, was the most popular* Log Cabin *arrangement in this seven-county area, followed by the* Barn Raising. *Most were constructed by pressing and sewing ascending lengths of strips to a foundation and then knotting or quilting that two-layer top to a filler and back hence the nomenclature of striped or pressed work. Some were pieced as is this example which has a nine patch block replacing the usual single colored central block of each unit. Red squares also are pieced onto the ends of each strip. These changes in*

technique add exciting visual elements to the piece.

Quilt by Mary Magdelena Guss Sieber b. 1829 Mifflintown, Juniata County d. 1921 Reedsville, Mifflin County. / Pieced calicos with plain back. Back brought to front as edge treatment. 97"×81½" with 8 stitches per inch. / Private collection.

In a note attached to this Double Nine Patch, *Jeanne Adams, the aunt of the present owner, wrote in 1957 about her grandmother, Mary Guss Sieber:* ". . . *patches began when she and brother Will watched cows together, when she was very small girl from bits she gathered that other sisters discarded. Red, larger patches of material her grandma bot for her a dress." The overall organization of this quilt and its fabric selection epitomizes the visual strength of dark quilts of*

simple pieced patterns that were made here in great number with scrap materials supplemented by store bought.

72

Quilt by Clara Leitzel Drumheller b. 1883 d. 1939 Snyder County. / Pieced calico and solid colored fabrics with print back. Applied solid colored binding. 82"×77" with 7 stitches per inch. / Collection of Isabel Drumheller.

Many of the area's pieced quilts from 1870-1920 are composed of dark fabrics exclusively. Many, like this, are organized around various arrangements of squares. This example was one of twenty-five quilts of Clara Drumheller's that were divided amongst her survivors after her death in 1939, Her collection of sample quilt patches also survives.

Dora Mensch Musser (extreme right) and Sarah Stahl Snyder (left) at a family gathering. Courtesy: Janice Snyder.

Joanna Beaver taken by Garber's Studio, Watsontown. Courtesy: Charles L. Beaver.

Quilt by Sarah Stahl Snyder b. 1889 d. 1968 Buffalo Township, Union County. / Pieced calicos with print back. Applied calico binding. 86¾"×76" with 6 stitches per inch. / Private collection.

Quilt by Joanna Beaver b. 1857 d. 1941 Limestone Township, Union County. / Pieced calicos with apron gingham back. Applied calico binding. 85¼"×69¼" with 6-7 stitches per inch. / Collection of Charles L. Beaver.

Both of these Union County Nine Patch quilts are typical of those seen. There were more nine patch quilts and their variations than any other pieced pattern in part, because it was a good basic design that was often a learner's first like Joanna Beaver's, but also because it could present challenges in color arrangement to even an advanced quiltmaker such as Sarah Stahl. According to family oral tradition, Joanna made the quilt when she was seven and blind from a bout with scarlet fever which would date it 1864. Its smallest squares measure 1½" across and form an overall patch of 10⅜" while the Stahl piece has its smallest square 2⅝" across making a patch of 8¼"

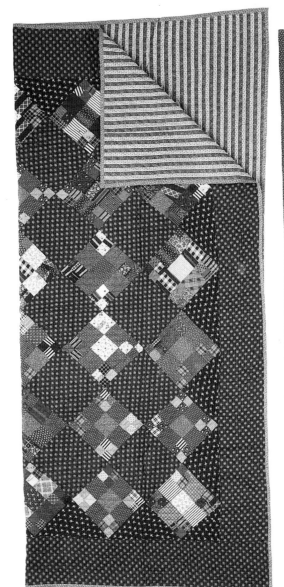

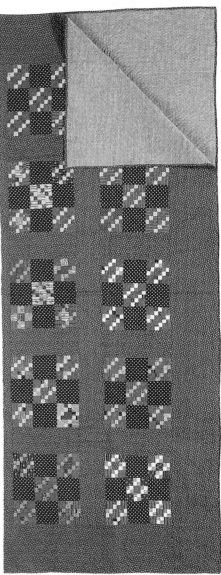

*Quilt by Sarah Haines b. 1838 d. 1934
Kelly Point, Union County. / Pieced
prints with plain back. Applied solid
colored binding. 78¹/₂"×77³/₄" with
9 stitches per inch. / Collection of
Karen S. Keiser.*

This Around the World *is one of many
quilts made as late as the 1920s by
Sarah Haines for her children and
grandchildren, and it is better
organized visually than most here. Its
individual squares measure 1³/₄" each.*

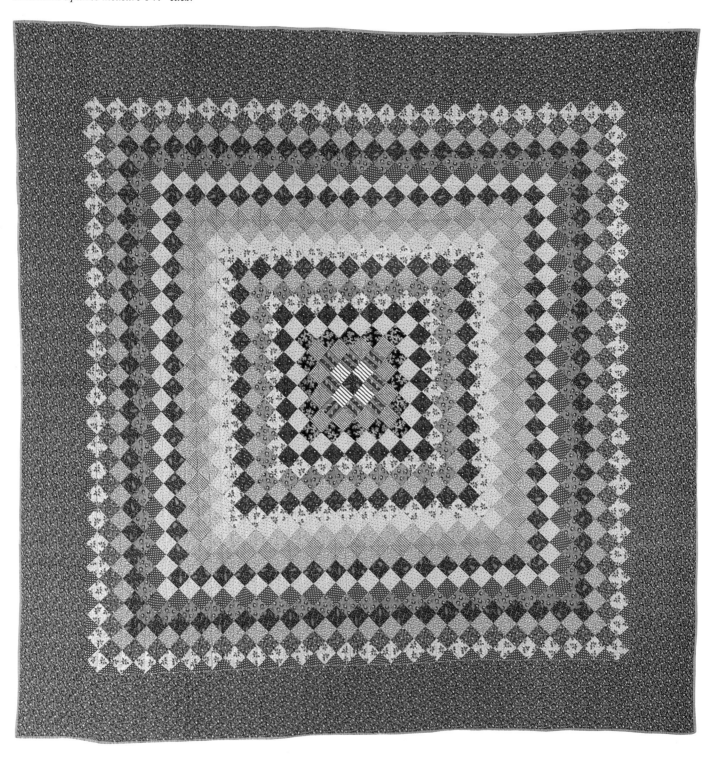

Milton, Northumberland County. / Pieced print and solid colored fabrics with plain back. Applied triangular pieced edge. 89"×87" with 6-7 stitches per inch in colored thread. / Private collection.

This is an area example of a great scrap quilt from the late Depression with well organized placement of solids and prints, each one inch square. One of its period names was American Tapestry. *It is finished with triangular pieces called "Prairie Points."*

I have found nothing so desirable for summer covers as the old fashioned scrap quilt, of which our mothers and grandmothers were so proud. They usually contain so little cotton that they are almost as easily washed as a sheet and can with very little trouble be kept sweet and wholesome, and last for years. When I say quilts, I do not mean the gay red, green and yellow abominations known as the "Rising Star" and "Setting Sun," that we see year after year exhibited at the annual country fair, but the modest "Hexagon," "Ninepatch," "Star", and "Irish Chain," that we were taught to make when we were "wee lassies" and sat plying our needles at mother's side. Every young girl should piece one quilt at least to carry away with her to her husband's home, and if her lot happens to be cast among strangers, as is often the case, the quilt when she unfolds it will seem like the face of a familiar friend, and will bring up a whole host of memories, of mother, sister, friend, too sacred for us to intrude upon.

"Beds, Bed Clothing and Bedmaking," by Annie Curd / *Good Housekeeping* / April 1888 / p. 290

Any beautiful quilts made by our grandmothers are now treasured possessions in the homes of today. There is a charm about the exquisite workmanship and quaint colorings that appeals to us, and it is not a matter of surprise that today there are still women who make their living by the quilting craft. Puritan housewives and pioneer maids were adepts at this work, and this needlecraft flourished all through the eighteenth century and continued to within the last forty years. Matrons of to-day tell us of the quilting parties they attended in their girlhood. These were social events, keenly looked forward to by young and old.

When the patchwork was completed and lined, it was placed in the quilting frame, which consisted of four bars of wood, ten feet long. The bars were crossed and tied firmly at the corners and the frame placed on the backs of chairs, thus enabling the quilters to sit around and do the quilting. When the quilt was finished as far as the hand could reach easily, it was rolled up on the bars and clamped again at the corners and continued until the center was reached.

Toward tea-time the husbands and brothers used to join the party, and a merry social time was then enjoyed. After tea the quilting was sometimes resumed, and the men helped or hindered by waxing the thread and threading the needles for the ladies.

In Colonial days the quilting parties served to break the monotony of the long winters and were extremely popular, for some people attended as many as thirty quilting parties in a winter. Much zest was given to them by the exchange of "calicoes," "polampours,"–India chintzes and high-priced French cambrics. They discussed designs and admired materials, and talked over the combinations of colorings with as much spirit as though it were a matter of state. The materials worked into these quilts bear little resemblance to the cheap, anilin-dyed calicoes of today, for many of them have survived a generation of wear, and their coloring is as beautiful as the day they were made into patchwork.

The amount of time spent in careful fitting, dainty design, intricate stitches and elaborate quilting that went to make the patchwork quilts can hardly be credited, but the women of that day reveled in the work and therefore we need not pity them. A beautiful quilt in the possession of an old Quaker family in Germantown was made from the pieces of silk supplied by the maker of Friends' bonnets. This coverlet looks like the back of a dove, with the soft grays and tans and ivories of which it is made.

Quaint descriptive names were given to the various patterns, such as "Log Cabin," "Job's Trouble," "Rising Sun," "Dove in the Window," "Crows' Feet," "Love's Knot," and such floral names as "Dutch Tulip" and "Rose of Sharon."

The making of the quilt was done in the following manner. The patterns for the patchwork were first cut out of stiff pasteboard and the pieces of material cut by the patterns. As every scrap was used up, many quite small patterns had numerous seams which hardly showed when the quilting came over them. The making of the top of the quilt would be the fancy work of months, but the interest never seemed to flag.

When the patchwork was completed it was laid on the lining with layers of wool or cotton wading between, and the edges were basted all around. It was then ready for the quilting frame. Many of these old-time bedspreads dispensed with the patchwork and were merely quilted. These were termed "pressed quilts" and were very often made in white and cream washing materials. They were often finished off with hand-made netted fringes, a work of art in themselves. Most intricate designs were employed in the making of these pressed quilts, and sometimes not a quarter of an inch of surface would be without quilting stitches.

In the earlier days a very laborious process of marking was resorted to. A string was dipped in thick starch and then was placed on the quilt and tapped so that the mark of the starch was impressed on the quilt. This left a faint line, that could be brushed off when the quilting was done. Later, different-colored chalks were used. These days of ready-marked materials for needlework and of practical methods of transferring patterns make us realize that the old-time methods must have been very tiresome.

When a counterpane has been quilted, it needs finishing neatly. There are several ways of doing this. The piece is taken out of the frame and laid on a large table and cut evenly on the four sides. The edges are turned in and seamed or bound in white, or, if it is a silk courre-pied, it is done with a pretty colored ribbon that harmonizes with the predominating shades. Sometimes when the quilt consists of a set pattern done in one solid color on a light ground, two or three inches of the dark shade is used for the border.

All kinds of fancy stitches were used to embellish the quilts—herring-bone, outline stitch and cross stitch. Sometimes a dainty little flower was worked in embroidery silk in each pattern, and again accent was given by a spot of dark color worked in silk. Occasionally a bold flower was outlined to bring it into strong relief. In fact, there was no end to the ideas and contrivances for making this handicraft original and distinctive.

In looking at old-time patchwork quilts, the day in which they were made can be told by the prints and calicoes that were used in their make-up. The old-time prints were certainly much more beautiful than those of to-day, but in the earlier Colonial days calicoes were scarce, and old woolen garments and worn-out flannel sheets and old coat linings were brought into service, after first being dipped in the family dyepot of old-blue or madder.

Quilt by Alice Swartz Baker b. 1873 d. 1960 White Deer Township, Union County. / Pieced calicos with apron gingham back, dated "1910." Back brought to front as edge treatment. 78"×76" with 6 stitches per inch. / Collection of Marvel L. Facer.

Union County. / Pieced calicos with apron gingham back. Applied solid colored binding. 80¾"×79" with 8-9 stitches per inch. / Collection of Dorothy and Donald Reiner.

Pieced quilts on the theme of "robbing Peter to pay Paul" are fairly numerous in this seven-county area. The idea was to take two small blocks of contrasting colors and cut them up into several components and then exchange some as seen in these two Union County examples. The Drunkard's Path was the favorite among these difficult patterns with twenty recorded, followed by the Orange Peel (7) and Hearts and Gizzards (5), a pattern first published in Godey's Lady's Book in October 1857 and called "patchwork." The patterns are difficult to piece because most had curved edges. Both of these quilts are backed with green apron gingham—one a check and the other a plaid. This was a particularly popular backing for quilts here from 1880-1920.

Alice Baker, her husband and pets. Courtesy: Gary Slear.

Long ago bits of stuff were sold in small bundles at country auction, and many were the keen bidders who bought up these remnants, which were usually woolen. Quilts made of washing materials were a later innovation.

It is like listening to a story to hear some old lady tell of "my daughter's wedding-gown" or "my son's cloak," all of which were worked into her beautiful old quilts.

"Old Time Quilting," by Mable Tuke Priestman / *The Designer* / October, 1910 / p. 372

Hap by Carrie Arnold Winegardner b. 1866 d. 1947 across the Snyder County line in Cocolamus, Juniata County. / Pieced solid colored fabrics with plain back. 74"×70" and knotted with black thread and embroidered with yellow feather stitch. / Collection of Mary and Robert Arnold.

The materials used in this hap as well as its bold heart image make the piece unusual. Corduroys and velvets on the top and flannel as the back were used on only a few quilts here.

Carrie Arnold Winegardner. Courtesy: Mary and Robert Arnold.

We have for a long time made our comforts by tacking them in quilting frames, and after adding as much cotton as we wish—which is generally four to six pounds—we draw our top straight and tightly over it. Have strong flax thread, double in a large needle. Have a pretty gay color of yarn that will contrast well with the color of the goods the comfort is made of. Divide the twist of yarn with the scissors where the hank is tied. Now run your needle down straight through your comfort where you wish a stitch. We take ours about four inches apart each way. Some like them tied a little further apart, and some nearer. As you go down through the comfort leave about three inches of the end of the thread on the surface. Now bring the needle up through again about half an inch from where you stuck it down. Lay the end of the cut skein of yarn about an inch through the stitch taken with the thread. Tie the thread in a firm knot, clip the ends closely, gather up the inch of yarn with the skein, and cut the skein off even with the other end, and you will have a pretty, fluffy rosette, with the ends of the thread well hidden. If you don't succeed at the first trial to your satisfaction you will by a few trials. We make all our comforts this way. Run the outer edges lightly together, and when they become soiled clip the thread that holds the rosette, rip the edges apart, wash the calico, then put the same rosettes back on them.

We like comforts made in this way better than quilted, because we can avoid the necessity of washing the cotton batting that is in them. Every person who has tried it knows how unsatisfactory a comfort is that has been washed with the cotton in it. Mattresses made in this way, with corn husks finely slit up, or of cotton batting, are nice on a spring bed for summer use.

"Making Bed Comforts," by Mrs. Throp / *The National Stockman and Farmer* / June 3, 1886

For a real winter comfort, large size, use four or five bats of good cotton which costs from fifteen to eighteen cents a pound. Cut a pasteboard four inches square, for a marker, and at each point of the square dot with a lead pencil indicating where to tie. This will insure exactness. Tie at these places with tidy cotton and tuft with Germantown yarn or zephyr. For a large comfort four ounces of zepher will be the amount required. A pretty finish is a crocheted edge or a large scallop drawn of with a small teacup and button holed with the same with which it has been tufted. Pink and blue make up prettily, but scarlet is more durable than any other color. . . .

White comforts are apt to soil at the top where they come in contact with the face, particularly if the spread is taken off at night, and this should always be done. To remedy this, take a width of cheese cloth making it as long as the comfort is wide, sew up the ends, slip over your comfort or blanket, making it secure by basting it on, or by means of little shield pins, which will come so far from the face, as not to inconvenience the sleeper. Have two for each bed, so that they may be washed as often as desired.

"Beds, Bed Clothing and Bed Making," by Annie Curd / *Good Housekeeping* / April 1882 / p. 290

To return to bedding. There is nothing better than good, home-made comfortables and quilts. Nothing really takes their place. One can buy fresh cottons and pretty prints, or cream or tinted cheese-cloth, and make bedclothes that are wholesome and can be easily washed. I must confess to being old-fashioned enough to like bedquilts, and to believe that while it is folly to buy calico and tear into bits for the same of sewing together again, that it is yet a pleasant pastime, a trifle of economy and a very satisfactory occupation to take the pieces of cambric and gingham which have accumulated, cut them in blocks, sew together on the machine, and make bedquilts of them. When these quilts are lined with some fresh, clean-patterned calico, with one layer of cotton batting between, and lightly quilted and neatly bound, they are joy to the thrifty housekeeper's eyes; they are easily washed, and on a hot summer night are infinitely preferable to stuffy blankets. Nor is it quite clear that there is anything reprehensible in making elaborate patch-work bed quilts. They are more useful than half the fancy work that encumbers houses, and if much of the petty gossip and idle tittle-tattle of society found vent in "rising sun" and "Irish chain" bedquilts I am not sure but that it would be a good thing. At all events, when our grandmothers were making "lover's puzzle" spreads for the spare chamber, they had their minds on their work, and were not going from home interesting themselves in their neighbor's business.

Good Housekeeping / March 1882 / p. 130

A nice way to use up worsted scraps of all kinds is to piece them as "crazy work" for a comforter. We made one this winter. Our blocks are about sixteen inches square; twelve blocks are sufficient for a pretty good sized one. Take old calico, or anything of the kind, to sew your patches on. The beauty of it is you do not have to cut them by any pattern. We worked the seams with yarn, all kinds of scraps were put into service, even some bright colored ravelings were used, and the comforter really does not look as though it were made of "cast-offs." I wish some of you would try it and report success.

"Make Use of the Scraps," by Lisena / *The National Stockman and Farmer* / February 28, 1889 / p. 916

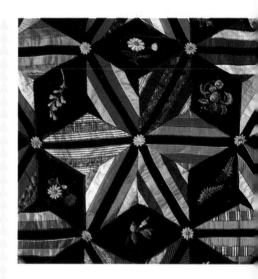

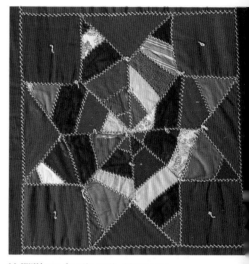

McWilliams family quilt, Shamokin, Northumberland County. / Pieced print and solid colored fabrics with plain back. Applied solid colored binding. 64¾"×51½" with various colors and stitches in embroidery floss. / Collection of Elva Sacona.

Centre County. / Pieced wools with plain back. Applied solid colored binding. 66" square knotted in white with overall yellow feather stitch. / Collection of Jean B. Smith.

These are two examples of strip star quilts. The McWilliams' quilt was made in the height of the crazy fad which lasted relatively briefly in the 1880s and 1890s. It was probably designed as a throw, not a warm bed covering, as was its counterpart found at a Centre County hunting cabin and which could have been made as late as the 1930s. This pieced wool comfort or hap is filled with wool backed by flannel, and is exceedingly heavy, meant to keep one warm in rooms that had little or no heat. Both pieces were made by sewing strips to a foundation material first, much like the Log Cabin *pressed construction types.*

A comfortable for a large or double bed ought to be three´yards long and three yards wide. You may make it of glazed coloured muslin, (in which case it cannot be washed,) or of furniture chintz, or cheap calico. It is best to have both the lining and the outside of the same material. Having run the breadths together, place it in a quilting-frame, and lay on the cotton bats thickly and evenly, each one a very little over the edge of the other. A comfortable of the above size will require three pounds of carded cotton bats. It should be quilted in very large diamonds, laid out with chalk and a long ruler, or with a cord line dipped in raw starch, wetted to a thin paste with cold water. In quilting a comfortable, you need not attempt to take close, short stitches.

The House Book, by Eliza Leslie / 1846 / p. 314

Says a housekeeper: 'My down satin-covered *comfortable* required cleaning and I determined to do it myself. So I made a good suds of the white soap and water not too hot, in which the quilt was soaked for an hour. After being rubbed gently with my hands, it was rinsed thoroughly and hung upon the line in the sun. To all appearances the comfortable was simply ruined, but I hoped for at least a little improvement when completely dried. At intervals I gave it a good shaking: and at the end of four days it was ready to be taken from the line. Had the manipulations improved it? Well it was so fluffy and beautiful after those four days of shaking and drying and sunning that I was going to say it looked even better than when new.

Good Housekeeping / April 1905.

Oh, say can you see by the dawn's early light
What you failed to preceive at the twilight's last gleaming;
A crazy concern that through the long night
O'er the bed where you slept was so saucily streaming;
  The silk patches so fair,
  Round, three-cornered and square,
  Gives proof that the lunatic bed-quilt is there.
Oh the crazy quilt mania triumphantly raves,
And maid, wife, and widow are bound as it's slaves.
On that quilt dimly seen as you rouse from your sleep
Your long-missing necktie in silence reposes.
And the filoselle insects that over it creep,
A piece of your vest half-conceals, half-discloses;
  There is Kensington-stitch
  In designs that are rich,
  Snow-flake, arrasene, point russe, and all sich.
Oh, the crazy quilt mania, how long will it rave?
And how long will fair women be held as it's slave?
And where is the wife who so vauntingly swore
That nothing on earth her affection could smother?
She crept from your side at the chiming of four
And is down in the parlor at work on another.
  Your breakfasts are spoiled,
  And your dinners half-boiled,
  And your efforts to get a square supper are foiled
By the crazy quilt mania that fiendishly raves,
And to which all women are absolute slaves.
And thus it has been since the panic began,
In many loved homes it has wrought desolation,
And cursed is the power by many a man,
That has brought him so close to the verge of starvation.
  But make it she must,
  She will do it or bust,
  Beg, swap, and buy pieces, or get them on trust.
Oh, the crazy quilt mania, may it soon cease to rave
In the land of the free and the home of the brave.

"The Crazy Quilt," *The National Stockman and Farmer* / January 8, 1891 / p. 904

It all came out of an idea that struck Heloise Herbert one day last winter.
 "You know I should never have ambition enough to begin a crazy quilt all by myself," she said to her mother. "But if Marie and I should undertake it together, we might finish it some time; that is, if—"
 Mrs. Herbert smiled at the breadth of this unspoken hypothesis, but the arrival of a letter relieved her from the responsibility of a reply. It was a fat, fashionable looking letter, written on terra cotta paper, in the scrawly, scrambling hand which swell young ladies affect.

My Darling Heloise, (it began, under a little Greenaway girl, holding a peacock feather,) *"I am delighted with your suggestion, and shall begin at once. This very afternoon I am going out to collect samples from the stores. Grandma has given me some lovely bits of old-fashioned brocade, and mamma says there are some scraps of silk up in the attic we can have. Of course I shall divide with you, dear. Don't let us have many large pieces in the quilt; the small ones are so much more effective. Janie Roberts has a sofa cushion made of tiny little bits worked up with spangles and gold thread, and it is quite oriental looking. I will write you what success I have. Excuse this hasty scrawl. With love, dearest, Yours always, Marie Atoinette Craig. Four, P.M.*

I have just returned from my shopping tour, and will enclose you half of the samples I procured. I met Dory down town, and we went to Blank's and had dinner together. When I showed him my silks, and told him what we were going to do, he said "Good heavens, Marie! you are not going to make one of those abominable things, are you?" (Did you ever hear anything so rude?) "I am going to make a crazy quilt, if that is what you mean," I said stiffly. "I am sorry for that," he exclaimed. "But I hope you won't make yourself a bore to your friends, Marie as some girls do. I don't want to see you plaguing men for their old neckties, and all that sort of thing." "I hope I know what is becoming to a lady," I said, with crushing emphasis. "But you won't do that, will you, Marie?" he persisted. "Promise me you won't. You don't know how the fellows make fun of these girls that go around begging for old silk—'rag-pickers' they call them." I felt myself getting very warm, and I let him have it. "I don't intend to beg," I said, cuttingly. "Most certainly, I shall not ask you for anything; but I shall get all the old neckties I can, and be thankful for them." Then we had it! He wanted me to promise, and of course I wouldn't. The very idea! I declare, the men nowadays think that because they are engaged to a girl they can demand anything they like. Dory was furious, and I don't think we'll ever make up again. He's so awfully jealous; I don't believe we could ever be happy together anyhow. Why I really believe, Lois, that he objects because he doesn't like me to have any man's neckties in my quilt except his! Isn't that ridiculous? Still I do wish he would be more reasonable. You know, I always did care more for Dory than for any other man I ever saw, and I can't be happy when we quarrel. Write me soon, dearest; I need your consolation. Yours disconsolately, M. Antoinette C.

Heloise answered this letter the following day, when she was down town and stopped in at her father's office to replenish her pocket-book.

"Poor Marie!" she murmured, as she took the desk which the clerk politely offered her, and laid her gloves and muff down alongside of a fat little bundle of silk samples. "I'm glad I'm not engaged or likely to be. In nine cases out of ten it makes life a burden. Thank you! That pen will do. I don't mind writing on business paper. It makes me feel quite important."

She took up the secretary's stub and poised it over the broad commercial sheet, while the perfume of violets drifted from her gloves and kerchief, she wrote as follows:

Dearest Marie:—I am awfully sorry about the trouble between you and Dory, but you mustn't let it worry you too much, for I am sure that it will all come out right in the end. You know how Dory acted up about you driving Charley Wheeler's dog-cart, and how he came around at last. Of course it is perfectly absurd of him, my dear; but what can you expect of a man?

Many thanks for your lovely samples. The storekeepers in Rochester are not so generous as they are in Albany. Some of them are awfully stingy; they only give you wee little mites of samples, and they cut button holes in them, so that they are of no earthly use. I will send you by this mail some that I got this morning. You know Emory Adams is head clerk at Hooper and White's now. Well, I went to him and told him that I wanted some samples of light brocade—I find the light colors are scarcer, don't you? He gave me a lot, lovely pieces, some four inches square, but would you believe it? They were every one pasted on bits of cardboard, so that I couldn't use them at all. Of course I didn't let on, but I was just too mad for anything! When I asked him what they did that for, he said that they were obliged to because there were some ladies—he supposed they call themselves ladies—who were mean enough to come there for samples when they didn't want to buy anything at all, but just use the silks for patchwork; that the firm had been driven to this expedient in self-defence. Isn't that absurd! As though a few little bits of silk could make any difference! "Of course, I know Miss Herbert, that you wouldn't do anything of that sort," he said, smiling, "but the innocent must suffer for the guilty." Wasn't that horrid of him? I shall never speak to Emory Adams again.

Have you done anything at your quilt yet? I have made two patches that are perfectly lovely. Ned says that we will never finish them, but we know better don't we, dearest? Ned is such an absurd brother! This morning he came in with a bunch of those nasty little yellow cigar ribbons all in a tangle, and offered them to me for my crazy quilt. But I don't intend to mind ridicule or any difficulties. Write soon and let me know how you are getting along; and tell me all about Dory. With much love, Your truest friend, Heloise Herbert.

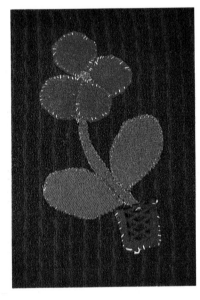

Hap by Alma Miller b. circa 1912 d. 1982 Paxinos, Northumberland County. / Pieced and appliquéd wools and felts. 60"×65" / Private collection. Photo: Bridget Allen.

Alma Miller, a solitary person who lived her entire life outside Paxinos, was always surrounded by a multitude of plants and animals. Their forms and colors were transposed by her through practical materials which she cut and sewed onto heavy fabric patches which she eventually made into four related bed coverings or throws. One cotton pieced sampler quilt of hers also exhibits the very individual approach she brought to her work.

P.S.—Tom Lee has given me a lovely silk handkerchief he has only carried a few times. Wasn't it sweet of him?   H.H.

The answer to this came on a finely written correspondence-card across one corner of which in embossed letters of a queer copper color was traced in script characters the word, *Saturday.*

"*Dear Heloise,*" it ran. "*Can't you come on and spend a couple of weeks with me while Mamma is in New York? I shall be horribly lonely, and we can do wonders at our quilts. Mamma has promised to bring me stacks of samples from New York. Aunt Annabel is going with her, for which heaven be praised. It is dreadful to have a rich aunt to whom you have to be agreeable whether you want to or not.*

"*I have just finished doing the little girl sitting on a fence. I did her in crimson etching silk on a bit of cream-colored satin, and she looks lovely. Mamma will bring us some new patterns from New York. I have sent begging letters to my friends out of town, and have had several contributions of silk. One old maid aunt sent me a whole silk dress, all of one pattern! She might have kept the ugly thing for dusters. I have been asking every lady who calls on me for a bit of her bonnet strings. Sometimes they give me several inches, and I find the pieces quite useful. No room for more. Good bye. Your own, Marie.*

Across the card was scribbled this one line: *Dory has not been near me.*

When this missive came, Heloise was sitting in a plush-covered chair, with her toes pertly perched on a shining brass fender.

"I wish I could go," she mused, as she took a few stitches in the cap of the little chocloate girl she was working on grey damassée. "Marie has begun on the opposite side of the pattern. If we were only together we could keep up with each other. But there is no use thinking of it now. What is it, James? Always knock, please. This came this morning, did it? From Hood and Blakeley. Why didn't you tell me? I always want these business communications answered at once."

The letter in question was written in copying ink and ran as follows:

Hood and Blakeley,
Dealers in Fancy and Dry Goods.
Rochester, Feb'y 10, 1883.

Dear Madame:—We do not furnish samples of silk except upon the deposit of five dollars as a proof of good faith on the part of the customer. If you desire samples on these terms, the amount of the deposit will be credited on your purchase.

We have been forced to this mode of doing business by the heavy expenses incurred in cutting up samples in compliance with the thousands of requests which we receive. Last year we cut up no less than nine thousand ($9,000) dollars worth of silks, and the salaries of sample clerks, etc., ran the annual expenses up to twelve thousand ($12,000) dollars, from a large proportion of which we had no return, as in only one case out of ten have we found customers among those who have applied for samples. Yours very truly, Hood & Blakeley, per J.V.R.

"Well," exclaimed Heloise, "the very idea! Nine thousand dollars! Pshaw! I don't believe it."

This is a woman's argument, but always suffices to strengthen her point of vantage, whatever the onslaught. If any misgivings came into Heloise's not really selfish heart, it was forgotten in the diversion created by a fashionable call.

"Oh, you are making a crazy quilt," exclaimed Mrs. Beacham Beauchamp, as she bent over the bit of growing patchwork. "What a pretty design. Where did you get it? From Godey's, did you say? What lovely things they do have! Where do you get your silks?"

"Oh, I don't know," Heloise replied. "A good many are given to me; then I get samples, of course, and—"

Mrs. Beauchamp burst into a rippling little falsetto laugh. "That reminds me," she exclaimed, pulling up her tan-colored mousquetaire gloves. "Last fall Mrs. Meredith and I— Dora Brown, you know—each made a crazy quilt, and such a time as we had getting our silks. We tried all the usual ways—old neckties, rag-bags, bonnets, and all that—and then we heard of the buyer's samples furnished by the American Silk Mills. We'd bought several lots of those cuttings they advertise, you know—you've seen them; you get so many for a dollar. But the buyer's samples are furnished free to large dry-goods firms, and Dora and I made up our minds to have some, and we got them."

"How did you manage it?" cried Heloise, eagerly.

"You musn't tell. Well, I'll confide in you, my dear. We just organized a fictitious firm, which we called Orr, Lane & Co.. You know I write a masculine hand anyway, and I conducted the correspondence. I wrote for buyer's samples, and they sent them on—lovely shades of fine silk and damassée and brocade, some of them six or eight inches square, and all bound together in a beautiful little book. Of course we had to pay the postage, but that was very little. We wrote five times, and they set us four books. The fifth time, they made no reply. I suppose they concluded that Orr, Lane & Co. were not very good customers."

Again Mrs. Beacham Beauchamp's laugh rippled gayly through the apartment, and Heloise joined in it. It is a curious fact that when a woman undertakes a bit of crazy patchwork, all natural compunctions seem to sink out of sight and mind completely.

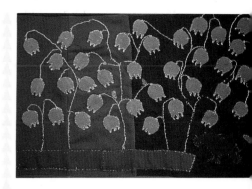

"That is quite an idea," Heloise said laughing; and when she wrote to Marie, telling her why she could not come to Albany just then, she suggested that they should try the same scheme.

"I have just gotten to that queer little zigzag piece in the corner," she wrote, "and I do want some kind of gay-figured goods for the next block. If you say so, I will get someone to write for us to the American Silk Mills. I have done the sunflower block in filosell. Mable has painted me some pansies, a bit of forget-me-not, and a spray of wild roses, which I shall put in somewhere. You know she paints beautifully. I tried my hand at it, but I mixed the colors in the evening, and having produced a brick-colored cabbage in place of a rose, and a crimson violet, I am not very proud of my achievements. Did you know that there is stamped muslin sold in the stores for a foundation for crazy patchwork? And you can buy lovely little figures to appliqué on in all colors. Janie Roberts is doing me a block with her monogram on it. But I must tell you what that ridiculous brother of mine is doing. He and Fred Townsend are making what they call a crazy quilt, too. The foundation is of coffee-bagging, and the blocks are made of old flannel shirts, stockings, linen collars, striped petticoats, aprons, bandanna handkerchiefs, etc., all cut in their proper form, and stitched on with pink, yellow, and purple wrapping cord. I asked Ned what they were going to do with it, and they said it was to be raffled off for a horse blanket at the firemen's fair."

But Marie was not in a mood to enjoy her friend's letter.

Dear, Darling Heloise, (she wrote in reply). *It seems very hard that you cannot come to me just at this time, when I need you so much! All is over between me and Dory forever. I broke off my engagement with him definitely last night, for I am convinced that we cannot make each other happy. To begin with at the beginning: After that quarrel we had at Blank's (I wrote you all about it), he never came near me till last night. Of course, I was not wearing the willow, and had been flying around a good bit with Charley Wheeler. Charley came to call on me last week, and he had on a lovely tie, one of those white Ottoman ones, with gold dots on it. I remarked: "What a lovely patch that would make for a quilt!" Of course, I didn't mean anything, for I never dreamed of his giving me a brand-new tie. "Would you like to have it, Miss Marie?" he said. "Yes indeed," I answered, for I thought he was just fooling. "I would give it to you," he said, "but I can't go home without a necktie. Wait a moment—give me the sissors!" And before I knew it, Heloise, he had cut all the portion of the tie that was hidden by his vest. I scolded dreadfully, but it was too late to stop the extravagant fellow, and all I could do was to promise to put the scarf in a prominent place. I worked it in on Saturday, and, more for fun than anything else, I embroidered on it a crimson heart pierced with a golden arrow. Last night Dory called. He came to make up, I knew, and he wanted just to ignore our quarrel entirely, but I wouldn't have it that way. My patchwork was lying on the table when he came in. "Isn't this pretty?" I said, carelessly, holding up the piece I had just finished. He recognized Charley's necktie at once, for there isn't another one in town like it. "Where did you get that?" he asked, quickly. "Charley Wheeler gave it to me," I said sweetly; "wasn't it good of him? It's the end of his new tie." Dory strode up and down the room for a few moments, and then asked fiercely: "What do you mean by working that upon it?" (tapping the heart and arrow with his finger). "Ah!" I exclaimed. "That's a delicate question." Then he flew into a passion, matters went from bad to worse, we quarreled and called each other names. I gave him back his ring, and and told him I never wanted to see him again. So now we have separated, and I feel very, very, wretched. Dear Heloise, do write me a comforting letter! You can do as you please about sending for the buyer's samples. I'm afraid I shan't be in the mood to work on the quilt for some time. Your disconsolate Marie.*

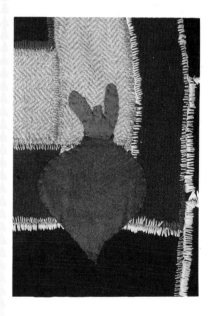

P.S.—Papa was in a fearful rage this morning because I cut the lining out of his spring overcoat. I didn't know he wanted to wear it anymore. I found it on the attic stairs and the sleeves were lined with lovely rose-colored striped satin, which I cut out. When he went for it this morning to take it to the scourer's and have it done up for spring, he found out what I had done, and we had a fearful scene. Oh, dear! I think I am the most unhappy girl alive. I wish I'd never begun this crazy quilt.
M.A.C.

Heloise wrote a prompt note of sympathy on fashionable, ragged-edged paper, but it was ten days ere she replied to Marie's letter in the following terms:

My Dearest Friend:—If your path has been strewn with thorns, mine is not much more inviting. I wrote the letter to the American Silk Mills, and signed it J.S. Osgood & Co. The book was to be sent to our box, but I received no reply till this morning, when James informed me that there was a gentleman in the parlor to see me. He gave his name

Quilt by Elvina Harter b. 1839 Nittany
Valley, Centre County d. 1921 Lock
Haven, Clinton County. / Pieced and
appliquéd silks and velvets with a
variety of colors and stitches in
embroidery floss. 74"×72". / Collection
of Peggy Stouck Petrucci. Photo:
Lance Ferraro.

Elvina Harter was a widow and living
in Lock Haven with her son and
daughter-in-law when she made this
quilt which was then exhibited at the
1904 St. Louis Exposition where it won
a third prize. Its surface is covered with
a lavish amount of embroidery and
incorporates many of the same motifs
seen on other area crazy quilts: spider
webs, horseshoes, flowers, crescent
moons, a flag, butterflies, and a fan.
What is unusual is the thousands of
beads she sewed over the entire surface
and the fact that her crazy blocks are
set within a sash which was not done
on any of the other one hundred and
thirteen seen.

and I was very much surprised to find an extremely handsome man in an elegant costume, waiting to see me. He looked at me with some surprise, and glanced from my China silk morning gown to the new ormulu cabinet. "Can I be mistaken?" he said, hesitatingly. "Is this Miss Herbert." "Yes," I replied. "Miss Herbert, who represents the firm of J.S. Osgood & Co.?" he continued, and the corners of his mouth took a peculiar turn. I felt my face growing scarlet. "I—I—believe—" I stammered, and could say no more. "You wrote to the American Silk Mills for a book of buyer's samples," he went on in the most provokingly cool tones. "Excuse me! My name is Johns, and I am here in the interest of the owners of the American Silk Mills. We are constantly receiving orders for sample books, and, as we supply them at a heavy expense to ourselves, the firm deemed it advisable, at the beginning of the year, to send some one to inquire into the commercial standing of such parties as may—" "There is no such a firm as J.S. Osgood & Co." I blurted out, for I began to get dreadfully frightened. "So I have found out," he answered quietly. "But you are aware that you have practiced a criminal deception using such a name to obtain what does not belong to you? If the firm saw fit to prosecute—" "Oh, I didn't mean anything," I screamed, "it was only for a crazy quilt. I did not think there was any harm in it. You won't—you can't arrest me. My father would never get over the mortification of it. Oh sir! I am very sorry! If money will do anything to—to—" Here I lost all control of myself and burst into tears. Then his whole manner changed toward me. "I was very much surprised to find that a lady in your position," he began—"I did not think you—" "No I didn't!" I answered quickly, "I didn't mean to do anything wrong." "You have been very foolish," he said, biting his lip, and then he burst out laughing. "Pardon me, Miss Herbert," he said, "but it is too ridiculous! The idea of a young lady's stooping to such devices to get patches for a crazy quilt, when she can perfectly afford to buy all the silk she wants." "But that isn't the same thing," I protested. "There is a great deal of excitement in collecting them." "I should think so," he said, still laughing. "But what are you going to do about it?" I urged. "Well, I don't know," he said. "Perhaps I can hush the thing up; but you must co-operate with me. I shall be in Rochester some time. You must not deem it an impertinence, if I call upon you." "No, assuredly not," I said, "you are very kind. If you can help me out of this scrape, I shall be forever indebted to you." "You want me to abet a swindle?" he said, smiling; "Well, you may count on me." I gave him my hand, and he held it consciously for a moment. "And I will see what I can do for you in the way of samples," he added. "Good morning." When he had gone, I felt dreadfully, for I seemed to realize for the first time what a mean thing we were doing in trying to cheat the shopkeepers. Besides, if it hadn't been for Mr. Johns' kindness, I might have been publicly disgraced. I feel grateful to him, but I am ashamed to look him in the face. Yours with discomfort, Heloise Herbert

A demoralized letter from Marie passed this one on the way.

Dear Lois: (it ran) *I am not going to try for any more samples or bits of silk. If what I've got already won't do, my quilt can go unfinished. Papa said this morning that I was making myself a nuisance to everybody, and if I didn't stop this sort of thing, he'd put my quilt in the fire. This sort of thing means, that while Mamma and Aunt Annabel were in New York, I went up in the attic, and found an odd silk sleeve of crimson brocade. It was just what I wanted, and, as it didn't seem to belong to anything, I cut it up into patches. Then Aunt Annabel comes home and raises the roof because I have cut up the sleeve of a dress she is making over! How was I to know that the sleeve was carried up to the attic by mistake? I shall never hear the last of it. Aunt Annabel was so mad she said she was going home. I wish she would go! Mamma says she will certainly cut me out of her will; but I'm sure I don't care. I haven't done a stitch at my quilt since I wrote last. Hastily yours, Marie Antoinette C.*

P.S.—Dory Willis is away on a business trip.

Heloise wrote promptly in answer to this:

My Dearest Marie: What you want is a pleasant change. Pack up your things, quilt and all, and pay me a visit. We can work together, and it will do you good to talk over your troubles. I do not want to give up my quilt, because I said so positively I would finish it at all hazards. Mr. Johns has been very kind. He sent me three lovely buyer's books on his own account, and says he will make the other matter all right with the firm. But he has told me so many things about the sample trade, that I feel very much like a swindler. Perhaps it will please you to know that I was properly introduced to Mr. Johns at Mrs. Vanderver's reception the other night. His first name is Archie. I would like you to meet him. Can't you come next week, or the week after? Let me know at once. Yours lovingly, Heloise

P.S.—I am away ahead of you with my quilt. I have just put the little boy in on a bit of sulpher satin. I worked him in black. If you come, I will help you with yours, so we can both keep together. H.H.

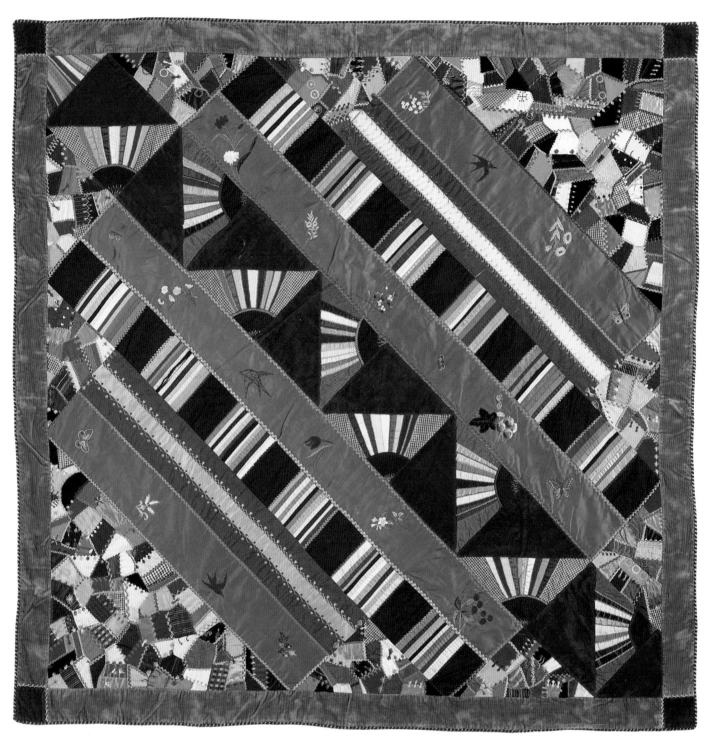

*McWilliams family quilt Shamokin,
Northumberland County. / Pieced
ribbons, silks, satins, and velvets with
plain back. Applied roping as edge. 73"
square with various colors and stitches
in embroidery floss. / Collection of
Jennifer Garcia.*

Mifflin County. / Pieced silks and velvets with machine quilted solid back. Back brought to front as edge treatment. 66" square with various colors and stitches in embroidery floss and painted images. / Collection of Sarah G. Ward.

In the height of the Victorian era, images were sewn, embroidered, and painted on a variety of surfaces including the high style crazy quilts such as these. The one is covered with objects, both very small and quite large, all of which are painted. They include anchors, crescent moons, bugs, ferns, dogs, many cats, horseshoes, fans, owls, cherries, butterflies, fish, a pear, birds: a chicken, heron, warbler, and swallows, a frog, roosters and rabbits. Human figures include a baby in a carriage, a girl with muff, one with a bird, one lifting a cat, one in a bonnet as well as a man with a hat and another at an easel.

Reed family quilt, Reedsville, Mifflin County. / Pieced and appliquéd silks and ribbons with plain back. Back brought to front as edge treatment. 60" square with various colors and stitches in embroidery floss and some painted images. / Private collection.

Quilt by Mary Ellen Fisher Fulmer b. 1841 Allenwood, Union County d. 1940 Williamsport, Lycoming County. / Pieced velvets, silks, and ribbons with machine quilted back, dated "1892" and "1893." Applied red, white and blue ribbon. 81"×79½" with various colors and stitches in embroidery floss and painted images. / Collection of David Frank Fulmer.

When Mary Fulmer died in July 1940, she left over ninety quilts to be divided amongst her relatives. This crazy quilt, with blocks from forty-eight states plus the District of Columbia, was amongst them. Some of the squares are dated "1892" and "1893" and it was probably put together soon after that. Utah, Oklahoma, New Mexico, and Arizona were still territories. Many of Mary Fulmer's quilts were done at group quiltings at the Redeemer Lutheran Church in Williamsport and quite possibly it is through the church's network with other churches that Mary accumulated the squares from such distances.

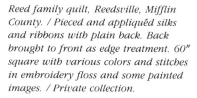

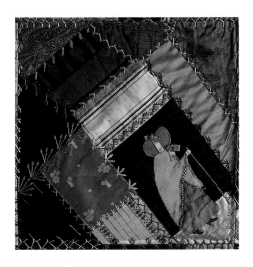

This was the last letter Heloise wrote about the quilt, for Marie replied that at the end of a fortnight she would visit her friend in Rochester.

It was a fair, sweet day in early spring that Heloise drove down in her phaeton to meet the 5:40 train.

Marie alighted in a pretty pongee traveling suit, richly trimmed with brown velvet.

"Oh, I am so glad to see you," said Heloise effusively, giving her a hearty squeeze. "But how pale and sad you are looking, dearie. You must get some color in your cheeks. This will never do."

"They tell me I am working too hard over my quilt," she said with a pathetic little smile, "and I shouldn't wonder if it would be the death of me yet."

"Oh I guess not," said Heloise, as she drew up the linen lap-robe, and a pleased, conscious look shone in her eyes—a look that Marie did not see. "Go right upstairs, dear," she said, when they reached the Hebert mansion. "That's right, the first room to the left."

"Oh, how lovely it is here," cried Marie, sinking into a cozy chair. "And why Lois, is that your quilt?"

"Part of it. Isn't it lovely? Don't dare to say yours is prettier."

"It isn't. The colors are arranged somewhat differently, but the effect is no better. How cute that little dog is. I haven't finished mine yet."

"There! Don't look at it any more, Marie, I want you to go downstairs. You know we are our own housekeepers. Papa has gone to Syracuse to the convention, and mamma went with him; they won't be home till day after to-morrow. Here are some roses for you. Put them on, and come down in the library when you are ready."

"How lovely!" cried Marie, as she buried her face in the dewy fragrance. "That was very sweet of you, dear."

Heloise gave her a little twinkling smile and vanished. Marie came down presently, fresh and sweet, with roses nestling on her bosom. As she raised the portière, she started back with a low cry.

"Dory!"

"Darling!"

He came towards her swiftly, with outstretched arms.

"You wear my roses," he said eagerly. Is that a sign that there is peace between us?"

"Your roses?" she faltered. "I did not know they were yours. But how came you here?"

"My friend, Archie Johns, sent me word you were coming. Marie, I have been wretchedly unhappy; there is a fault somewhere. I am not quite sure who is most to blame, but I am sorry for my side of the quarrel. Will you forgive me?"

Marie could not withstand this. She flung her arms around his neck, and sobbed out upon his breast:

"Oh Dory! I have been so unhappy! I just hate that old crazy quilt, and I never want to see it again!"

Then a long silence transpired, a silence broken only by soft whispers and a gentle osculatory sound that disturbed no one. After a while—it may have been moments or it may have been hours—the portière was swept aside, and Heloise surprised the two lovers in the midst of a fervid embrace.

"Tableau!" she cried, mischievously.

"Reflection!" cried a mellow voice at her elbow, and in the same moment she herself was imprisoned in somebody's arms.

"Archie Johns!" she said, struggling and blushing furiously, "aren't you ashamed?" "Why, Heloise!" Marie exclaimed in confusion, "I did not know that—that—"

Then everybody laughed in a foolish way, and it was several moments before Heloise had the presence of mind to say:

"Marie, this is my affianced husband Archie Johns. Archie, this is my dearest friend, Marie Craig, my fellow patchworker."

This interesting scene was terminated by the ringing of the tea-bell. As Heloise and Marie went out to the dining-room, leaning on their lover's arms, Ned, who was leaning on the banister, uttered a prolonged "Whew!"

There is little more to tell you know. Archie Johns contracted to supply the young ladies with all the silk they might need to finish their patchwork, and the two crazy quilts were done in time for the double wedding that took place last fall.

For sentiment's sake, Marie gave her quilt to Heloise, and Heloise gave hers to Marie. Both quilts were finished with a beautiful rose-colored border, on which were worked the following lines:

"All precious things, discovered late,
To those that seek them, issue forth;
For love in sequel works with fate,
And draws the veil from hidden worth."

"The Career of a Crazy Quilt," by Dulcie Weir / *Godey's Lady's Book* / July 1884 / pp. 77-82

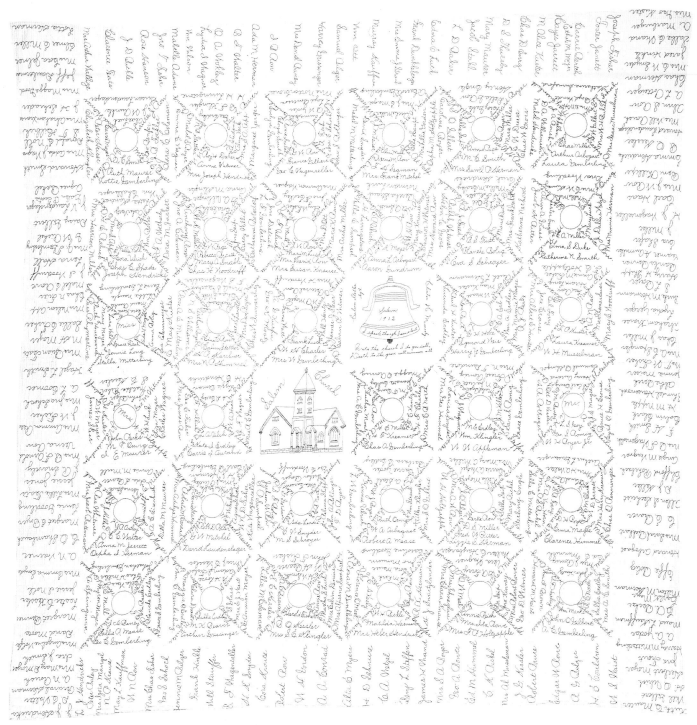

Salem, Snyder County. / Embroidery
on white top with plain back, dated
"1902." 83"×82" with 8 stitches per
inch. / Collection of Lila and
Calvin Witmer.

Seven hundred and forty signatures
were embroidered in Turkey red thread
as part of a fundraising effort for the
Salem Church in Snyder County in
1902. The spoked design is one
typically used on quilts of this type but
the embroidered images and sayings
are not: "I speak though I am silent"
on the bell and "Unto the church I
do you call/Death to the grave will
summon all" below it. This quilt is one
of approximately a dozen area
fundraisers seen.

*Quilt by Verna Felmy Miller b. 1890
Franklin Township, Snyder County d.
1970, Mifflinburg, Union County. /
Pieced print and solid colored fabrics
on white top with plain back. Applied
white binding. 78¼"×76¾" with
7-8 stitches per inch. / Collection of
Ellen M. Spangler.*

The Double Wedding Ring *along with
others like the* Broken Star, *the* School
House, *and* Sunbonnet Sue *were
patterns that were introduced into the
quiltmakers' repertoire relatively late in
the history of the craft. It became quite
popular in the early twentieth century
in spite of its piecing difficulty and
some women cite it as their favorite,
making it repeatedly. Verna Miller's
example is particularly pleasing in its
scale, its use of tan, and its overall
placement.*

*Verna Felmy Miller and her husband,
John on their anniversary. Photograph
taken by Elwood Moyer of
Mifflinburg. Courtesy: Ellen M. Spangler.*

Quilt pieced by Hester McAfee Mitchell b. 1894 d. 1980 Paxtonville, Snyder County and quilted by her mother Mary Jane Gift McAfee b. 1865 d. 1959 Paxtonville, Snyder County. / Appliquéd solid fabrics on white top with plain back. Applied solid colored binding. 79"×77" with 10 stitches per inch. / Private collection.

The favorite palette of pink and green calicos was later transposed into solid pastels of sateen cotton as seen in this finely executed 1920s quilt. The tulip pattern is the type promoted by Mountain Mist and other quilt pattern sources of that period. Its edges are finished in a fine blanket stitch as were many quilts from that time through the 1930s. Paxtonville had many women, like Hester McAfee Mitchell and Mary Jane Gift McAfee, who quilted both alone and in group quiltings at that time.

Photograph of Mary Jane Gift McAfee c. 1910. Courtesy: Kathryn G. Gift.

Pletcher family quilt, Centre County / Pieced silks with plain back. 44"×36½" / Collection of Centre County Library and Historical Museum.

Quilt by Viola Beahm Boyer b. 1875 d. 1947 Haines Township and Eva Boyer Rearick b. 1914 Haines Township, Centre County. / Pieced print and solid colored fabrics with plain back. Applied white binding. 78"×71½" with 11-13 stitches per inch. / Collection of Eva L. Rearick.

The pieced hexagon pattern is associated in many peoples' minds with the pattern name Grandmother's Flower Garden because of the great number of these done in the 1920s and 1930s. The basic pattern was illustrated over one hundred years earlier in Godey's Lady's Magazine as one recommended for silks. However, the hexagon quilt top was done here in cottons early as well, as seen in the work of Eliza Brown McLaughlin of Lewisburg. The major difference between the early to mid-nineteenth century examples and those of the twentieth century is to some extent the fabrics but primarily their organization. The later ones were made of pieced units which were then unified by a hexagon of a single color, often called a path. The Boyer quilt has approximately 4,518 pieces each ⅝" connected by a white path while the Pletcher piece is composed of hexagons ½" long on each side some still with their paper templates.

Viola, Eva, and Newton Boyer in 1935. Courtesy: Eva Boyer Rearick.

Quilts by Clara Nestlerode Hunter b. 1864 d. 1944 Beech Creek, Clinton County. / Pieced print and solid colored fabrics with plain backs. Applied white binding; back brought to front as edge treatment. 87"×71" with 8 stitches per inch; 87"×75½" with 7 stitches per inch. / Collection of Mrs. Nellie E. Lucas.

These scrap quilts are typical of those being made here from the late 1920s until 1940. The star pattern harks back to earlier quilt tops where pieced patterns touch each other covering the entire surface only to be framed by a sawtooth border, while the Basket of Scraps *or* Rainbow Cactus *is more indicative of the new trend where pieced patterns were placed on a large expanse of white without the benefit of a sash or border.*

Clara Nestlerode Hunter. Courtesy: J. Frederick Hunter.

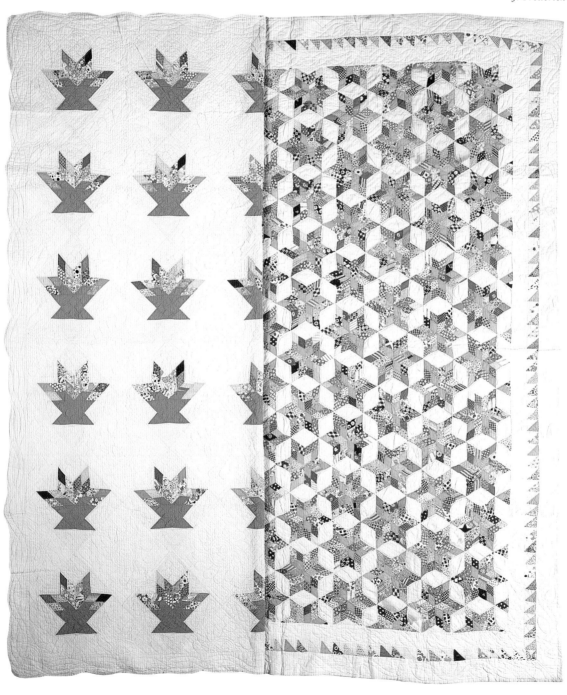

*Quilt by Ruth Harter Smeltzer b. 1894
Jacksonville, Centre County d. 1973
Lock Haven, Clinton County. / Pieced
print and solid colored fabrics on white
top with plain back. Back brought to
front as edge treatment. 72" square
with 6-7 stitches per inch. / Collection
of Mrs. Emogene Smeltzer Williamson.*

*Thousands of scrap triangles make up
this large star made by Ruth Harter a
number of years after her marriage
to Harry Smeltzer in 1912. The pattern
had never been seen until the quilt
documentation day in Lock Haven
where two were brought in within
minutes of each other.*

*Ruth Harter Smeltzer. Courtesy: Mrs.
Emogene Smeltzer Williamson.*

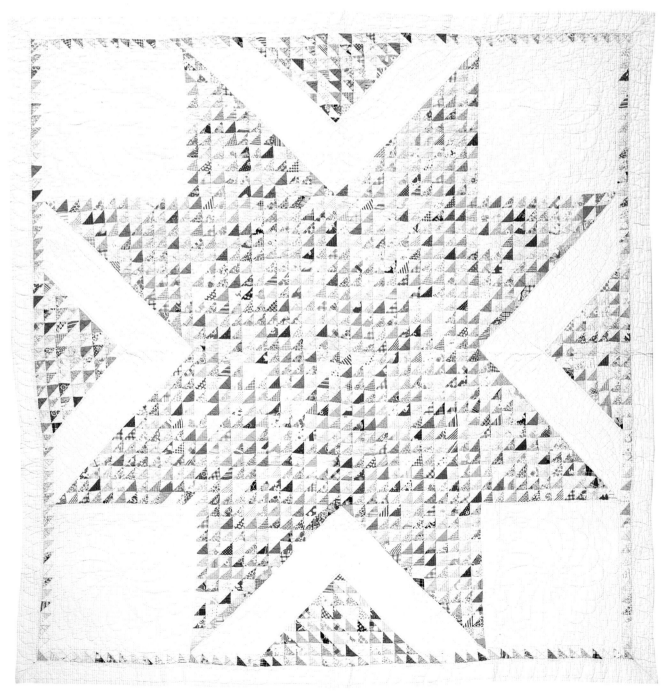

The pattern given is suitable either for a bed quilt or bassinet cover, and is of a proper size for working. In doing patchwork, care must be taken to cut all your papers of the exact size; after which baste your silk (or whatever material you are using) over the papers; and when you have a quantity so covered, choose your colors to harmonize; after which, connect the edges by sewing very closely and even, leaving the papers in until the whole is put together; after which, undo the basting-stitches, pick out the papers, line the work with glazed calico, and quilt it in any pattern you please, so as to keep the lining and cover tight together; or it may be knotted in the centre of each star, with any bright-colored floss-silk or Berlin wool.

Godey's Lady's Book / September 1854 / p. 269

This is a day of autograph hunters. The epidemic assumes various forms. Some have the craze for postal albums. One lady of my acquaintance has an album of several hundred postals from people she admits she never saw, and never expects to see. Another rage is the autograph quilt, but few people at present have the temerity to aspire to the crazy quilt. For my part I have not yet been able to decide whether I like them or not, I have seen so many witched and bewitched into what was originally intended to be a thing of beauty, but what really seemed more the production of the weakened brain of some poor aesthetic lunatic. In fact I never see a crazy quilt without a vivid childhood remembrance of a kaleidoscopic view I once had after falling from a high swing. Autograph quilts containing a block from each state and territory in the Union are also much in vogue. My idea of an autograph quilt is something entirely different, and as it is original with myself I will give it, as it will no doubt be new to others. I am saving a piece of each dress and apron of my children's clothes from their babyhood up. Upon each piece I fasten a bit of paper with the date and age of the child at the time they had the garment. After I am done collecting I shall make each a quilt of his and her own pieces, then with indelible ink mark each block the age of the child at the time the garment was bought, also what the garment was. What think you of my idea? Try it, mothers. It will be something the children can always keep, and something they will prize above gold long after that dear mother has crossed the mystic river into the great beyond. I love to piece quilts, and expect to be just that old-fashioned all my life.

"Autograph Quilts," by Mrs. F.A.W., East Saginaw, Michigan/*Good Housekeeping*/October 26, 1889/p.311

Quilts and comfortables are not adapted to the sick-bed, on account of the difficulty of thoroughly cleansing or disinfecting them. Sheets, blankets, spreads—these can be washed and perfectly purified; but with the comfortable the case is quite different. In the first place, the loose cotton with which it is padded is extremely absorbent, and is naturally adapted to take up and hold the germs of the disease. This is a fact which should not be lost sight of in the consideration of the desirability of the cotton-filled comfortable. Not that it should never be used, though it is a question whether the advantage would not be on the right side, if it were entirely abolished. But its use should be confined to the beds of people in good health, large children or adults; and it should have frequent thorough airing and full exposure to the sunshine. Thus used during the coldest of the season, homemade quilts and comfortables have a place of utility.

Good Housekeeping / June 1894 / p. 264

The time was when patchwork quilts represented merely the odds and ends of the piece bag, when, from the remnants left over from frock or apron, squares and cubes were cut to keep the housewife busy, to teach the little girls to sew, and to make the outside of a quilt, which, after completion, would add to the stock of winter bed coverings. But nowadays the patchwork quilt is most often made from material specially bought for the purpose, and usually only one color and white are used.

The designs for patchwork quilts given on this page may be made from patches of either silk or cotton, tiny pieces of either of these materials being just the things required for these patchwork quilts. When made of the latter, care must be taken to select only the colors that will stand repeated visits to the laundry. Turkey red is always safe, and there is also a blue cotton, which may almost be called Delft in color, that is effective and safe to use.

"Designs for Patch Work Quilts," by Fane Benson, *The Ladies' Home Journal* / November, 1896 / p. 24

The truly economical gets all the wear possible out of everything. For example, she wears her gowns until frequent makings over have not left enough cloth for another renovation unless for a smaller person. After doing duty there she pieces them into comforts. When they grow shabby she either covers anew at the worn edges, or by putting two together makes a comfortable summer mattress for bed or cot. She never gives then to her husband for horse blankets with a certainty of their being torn to pieces in a week. One comfort folded into three thicknesses makes a very nice mat for a hammock, particularly one made of slats. On ironing day it saves the feet from aching by forming a soft place to stand on. When three persons are obliged to ride in a single carriage this same mat is rolled up and placed between the two occupying the seat, and the third person sits on the mat; thus all have comfortable seats.

The National Stockman and Farmer / August 18, 1898 / p. 15

The fashion has prevailed for many years of dressing beds all in white has no doubt caused the destruction of many beautiful quilts. The white quilts that have been preserved are now considered too valuable to be subjected to hard wear. The most exquisite ones were made in the last of the eighteenth and the beginning of the nineteenth centuries.

It was the rage for white bed coverings that shortened the lives of many old pieced and patched quilts of good colouring. The "Country Contributor" tells of her experiences in dressing up the white beds:

"I remember with regret the quilts I wore out, using them white side up in lieu of white Marseilles spreads. The latter we were far too poor to own; the 'tufted' ones had worn out; and I loathed the cheap 'honeycombed' cotton things we were forced to use unless we were going to be frankly 'poor' and cover our beds with plain patchwork, made up hurriedly and quilted in simple 'fans' in plebeian squares, as poor folk who haven't time for elegant stitches did theirs. So I used the old quilts, making their fine stitches in intricate patterns serve for the design in a 'white spread,' turning the white muslin lining up. A beautiful white spread it made, too, I realize now, more fully than I did then, though I now would know much better than to turn the wonderful applique stars and flowers and wheels from view."

Quilts/Their Story & How To Make Them, by Marie Webster / 1926 / pp. 87-88

Day by day, the magic and beauty of Colonial America is making its way into the modern house.

Olde Kentucky Quilts are a delightful result of this desire to recapture the charm of Early American house furnishings.

No quest for antiques is more eagerly pursued today than the quest for quilts— the uniquely patterned and brightly colored bed coverings that were the pride of our grandmothers.

Unfortunately, few of the old quilts remain. Fortunately, the finest of the old treasures have become models for Olde Kentucky Quilts. So that now, at a very moderate cost, every bedroom in your house may be fitted with its own particular pattern and color.

Olde Kentucky Quilts are rich in tradition and are true to their noble ancestry. Each design is faithfully copied from an antique quilt.

The materials are fine sateen or good, soft-finished cotton cloth. A filling of fluffy new cotton makes the quilts soft and warm. Every one is wrapped in an individual glassine paper package. Colors are tub-fast.

Examine the lovely patterns shown on this page. Picture each of these designs in the various colors. The Turkey Foot design, shown on bed, is made in six colors. Imagine your bedrooms enlivened by these fascinating quilts.

Do you know the ancient origin of quilts? Do you know the history of your grandmother's treasures? A beautiful booklet, "Olde Kentucky Quilts," tells this romantic story. If your department store or furniture dealer cannot supply you, fill in and mail the attached coupon.

Louisville Bedding Company, Incorporated, Manufacturers, Louisville, Kentucky

Good Housekeeping / April 1928

Seventy-five years ago the world moved more slowly, and they had to find things to occupy their time. With a complete reversal of conditions, we now have to search for time to accomplish those things we want most to do. If, more than anything, you'd like to hand down to posterity a patchwork quilt, you can very easily do so by purchasing the patches ready cut, and sewing them together on a machine. The one in Figure 11 was made in that way in a single day, and you would, I think, like it immensely. Put together by hand, and further enhanced by quilting, it is as fine as anything your grandmother could have made. This is called the churn-dash pattern; it is made of two different shades of pink printed calico (sunfast) and unbleached cotton cloth. Finished, it measures 75″ × 89″. The unbleached cotton is supplied for the binding but not for the back, for it can be purchased anywhere. The price of the patches, ready cut, is $7.50, postpaid!—Patchcraft Corporation, 233 Fourth Avenue, N. Y. C.

House Beautiful / January 1929 / p. 9

The Designer, *November 1897*

Quilt pieced by Mary E. Iddings
b. 1912 West Buffalo Township, Union
County and quilted by Maude C. and
Lizzie Kaup b. 1886 d. 1962 and b.
1884 d. 1969 Buffalo Township, Union
County. / Appliquéd solid colored and
print fabrics with plain back. Front
and back turned in as edge treatment.
86" square with 8 stitches per inch. /
Collection of Mary E. Iddings.

The French Doll, Sunbonnet Sue, and
Colonial Girls were variations of new
appliqué designs which became popular
in the 1930s. As in this French Doll
done in sateen cottons, outline stitches
in contrasting embroidery floss,
French knots as buttons, and other
sewn details were customary.
Here, the girls' hands are pleated
three-dimensional forms not fully
attached to the quilt top in order to
give a semblence of realism. Similar
three-dimensional treatment was given
to the hankies of the Boys in Overalls a
quilt of the same era.

Mary E. Iddings. Courtesy: Mary E.
Iddings.

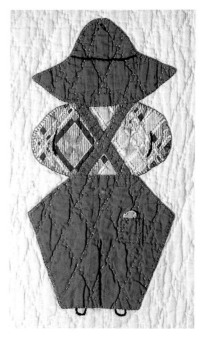

Quilt by Helen Everitt Pfleegor b. 1915 Milton, Northumberland County. / Appliqué of solid colored fabrics on white top with plain back. Applied solid colored binding. 85"×66¹/₂" with 8 stitches per inch and some embroidered work in colored thread. / Collection of Helen Everitt Pfleegor.

Two years before she was married, Helen Everitt, ordered her first quilt kit, The Lilies, *from the 1934 catalog of the Home Art Company in Chicago. The top and patches cost her $2.98, the blue back was $1.98 and the wadding was $.79. This was the first quilt, of many done in her family, to be made from a kit. The stitching in the front was marked to be quilted as water ripples.*

Helen Everitt. Courtesy: Helen Everitt Pfleegor.

Quilt by Gladys Dunkelberger Crone b. 1909 Trevorton, Northumberland County d. 1980 Elysburg, Northumberland County. / Appliquéd solid colored and print fabrics on white top with plain back. Applied white binding. 72"×47¹/₂" with 8 stitches per inch. / Collection of Donna Crone.

While living in Shamokin, Northumberland County, Gladys Crone made this quilt for her only child, Donna, born in 1941. Gladys had learned to quilt with her mother, Donna Dunkelberger, and her aunt, Lena Thompson, before going with her younger sister Jean to the group quiltings of the Ladies' Aid at the Irish Valley Methodist Church. They were allowed to quilt a few stitches but often had them ripped out until they could quilt more finely.

97

Quilters' Questionnaire

Name _____

Address _____

Phone No. _____

Birthdate and Place _____

Where Lived When Quilting _____

Ethnic Background _____

Date Information Taken _____

1. When and where did you first take part in anything that had to do with making a quilt?
   How old were you?
   What aspect did you do at first?
   After that, how frequently did you participate? In what ways?

2. Were your family members or friends quilting also?
   Who? When? Where?

3. Who taught you to make quilts?
   What did you think of them as people? as quiltmakers?

4. What pieced or appliquéd patterns did you do when you first started?
   What quilting patterns were your first?
   Did these patterns differ from your mother's or grandmother's work or . . . ?
   Did you prefer pieced or appliquéd work? Why?

5. How did you add to your repertoire of patterns: Trading with families or neighbors? from a kit? magazines (which ones)? personal invention? Seeing quilts at a fair? Other?

6. Were you aware of batting companies like Mountain Mist and others promoting quilt patterns and kits? Sears, Roebuck? The Ladies Art Company?

7. Which were your favorite patterns and why?
   Did this change over time?
   Did certain patterns remind you of past times or people?
   Any idea how quilt patterns got their names?
   Did any of your patterns go by another name elsewhere?

8. Did you have or see "sample" patches anywhere?

9. What colors did/do you prefer to use?
   What made you like them?
   Were you always able to get them?
   If you couldn't what would you do?
   Did you ever make an all-white quilt? For any special purpose?

10. Were your materials bought specifically to make a quilt?
    Were they remnants from sewing other items?
    Were they ever parts of discarded clothing? Ribbons? Neckties?

11. What was your source(s) for purchased material over the years?
    Did you feel limited or stimulated by their selection?
    Did you ever dye fabric to get the desired color?
    Did any colors tend to be dye eaten?

12. Any effects of new materials on quilt designs or palette?
    Did you use outing flannels? Feedbags?
    How did you learn to manipulate the colors needed in any given quilt?
    Were there any color rules?

13. What fabrics were desirable or undesirable? Why?
    Did this change over the years?
    Did quilts reflect fashion?
    Did you ever order sample patches of silk or velvet?
    Did you ever see a crazy quilt that was in cottons?

14. What would you consider unusual color combinations?
    Typical combinations?
    Who in your community did typical work and why?
    Who did unusual work and why?

15. Were your quilts among the most colorful items in your house?
    What else was colorful?

16. Did quilt patterns and/or colors pick up themes or colors from things around you? Examples:?
    Did pattern names reflect the landscape, politics, or religion, for example?

17. Describe how one planned a top.
    Did people ever sketch an overall design out before beginning?

18. Was there ever a tradition in your family or a neighbor's in copying quilts that had been done by past generations?
    Did "grandma's quilt" have a special place in your life? Mother's?

19. Were crazies used in different ways from quilts?
    What is a comfort? A hap?
    Do they have to be thick to be called that?
    Can a comfort or hap be quilted as well as knotted?
    Do they usually have wool inside?

20. What was used for your quilts' backing or foundation?
    What was used for the filling?
    Where was either purchased?
    Was the filling in bat form or otherwise?
    What was your filling preference and why?
    How did the filling affect the quality of quilting?

21. What were the criteria for good work: Design or color sense? Piecing accuracy? Intricacy? Needlework finesse? The shortness, closeness, evenness of the stitches?
    What would be the order of importance?

22. Who was known to do the best work in your community?
    Who did the greatest number of quilts and what was the number?
    Was there ever a local record for the number of pieces in a quilt?

23. Do you tend to want to look at a quilt from a distance or close-up? Hand held?

24. Were there any superstitions regarding quilting: when to quilt or when not to (Good Friday and Ascension Day)?
    Not quilting a heart until the bridal quilt, otherwise a spinster?
    Needing 12 quilt tops before engagement?

25. What would you do with old worn quilts?

26. In quilting were straight or blunt needles preferred?
    Bent ones?
    How did you break in a needle?
    What kinds and size of threads and needles were used?
    Was beeswax used for anything?
    Was anything used to stop the bleeding in case you pricked yourself?
    What was used to clean the blood from the quilt?

27. Did you ever use a sewing machine for any aspect of a quilt?
    Did you prefer a top sewn by hand or machine-sewn?
    Were there any taboos in using a machine?

28. What kind of templates (or patterns to be traced) were made for quilting designs?
    Who made them and how?
    Where were they kept?
    Were they ever destroyed?

29. How did you trace patterns: Did you starch templates and leave the starch outline on the top? Or did you trace around them with a pencil or chalk? Did you prick your design around their edge?
    Was one method preferable and why?
    Were these marks ever removed?
    Was anyone a marker of quilts in your area? What did they charge?
    Did you ever use a plate or cup for a basic quilting design?

30. Did you quilt away or towards yourself?
    Are you ambidextrous?
    Did you know anyone who was?
    How did you introduce new thread?
    How did you hide the knots?
    Did diagonal quilting hold better?

31. If there was more quilting was the quilt a warmer one?

32. How did you decide which quilting pattern to use?
    Were the different sections of the quilt, i.e.: border, rake, fill-in blocks, pieced blocks, each quilted differently?

33. Did you quilt alongside seams? Both sides of a seam? Regardless of placements of seams?
    Did you ever have a preference?
    Did you ever stuff quilting patterns? Ever hear of anyone doing that?
    Did you ever quilt in colored thread?

34. How many stitches did you get to the inch?
    What was the record amount heard of?
    Did your backs look as good as your fronts?
    How close were your rows of quilting?
    Did they become further apart? Any reason?

35. Did you have a special way to finish a quilt's edge?
    Was a separate edge applied?
    Homemade or store-bought bias tape?
    Was the front brought over to the back? Or the back to the front?
    Was piping ever used as trim as well?

36. What determined the quilting patterns in the border?
    The size of the border?
    A double border?

37. Did you quilt alone? At a bee? In the family only? With friends? At the church?
    Which did you prefer and why?
    Were most quilts in your area worked on alone or communally?

38. Why were quilts made? dowry / gifts (for whom) / mementos / strictly to use / as revenue / as a fundraiser?

39. Did people tend to make more quilts than they needed? Not enough?

40. Describe the activities of a quilting bee:
    Time of arrival
    Number of people
    What was expected to be done in how long?
    Meals or snacks—what was eaten and who would provide it?
    What did you talk about? children, taxes, recipes, weather, housekeeping or gardening tips, problems, etc.
    Who was invited; did it have to do with friendship or quilting abilities or proximity or something else?
    Would inferior work be ripped out and by whom? Who would decide to do that?
    Transportation to and from bee?
    Where were bees held?
    Did bees stop being part of the social scene? When?
    Feelings about bees in retrospect?
    Were other activities associated with bees: i.e. oyster supper, music, courtship, etc.
    Were there only women at the quilting bees? Men? Children? Describe the difference between public and private bees.
    Were some of these quilts used to raise money?
    For what groups?
    What groups quilted in your area?

41. Were there professional quilters in your community and how were they paid or how did they charge?
    Were they highly regarded?
    Was there any effect on their work because they were quilting for pay?
    What kind of work did they do: pattern range and quilting range?
    Did they only quilt?

42. Was there any aspect of rivalry in quilts? Examples:
    If you didn't like to quilt or did it poorly, were you thought less of?

43. Was there any place where quilts were judged locally: fairs, bazaars, etc.?
    Were prizes given and what were they?
    Who won them?

44. In preparing for a dowry, how many tops would or should be made?
    By oneself or others?
    When would they be quilted?
    How long would this supply be expected to last?

45. Did women tend to stop quilting during their early married life when they were raising a family?
    Did they resume and when?
    Whom did they quilt for then?

46. How many quilts did you do in a year?
    Additional tops?
    For whom?

47. What was the most pieces you ever put into a quilt?

48. Were any other objects quilted: pillowcases, pincushions, tabletops, or chair seats?
    Were some items pieced but not quilted?

49. Other than crazies, did you do embroidered quilts—white with Turkey red thread?
    Were they a range at a certain time?
    Yo-Yos?
    Ever hear of a stenciled quilt?

50. Did you ever do quilts that were primarily embroidered scenes on a solid background?
   Were your designs transfer or stamped patterns or designed by yourself?
   What was your embroidery thread called?

51. Was there such a thing as a "show quilt"? How was it used and when?
   What patterns and colors were most often used for show quilts?
   Did any of these show quilts have covers?

52. Ever hear of a centennial quilt? A Union quilt?
   Any particular patterns?

53. Did you ever make a friendship quilt? For whom? What pattern?
   How often was this done in your community?
   Did this practice flourish at any one particular time?
   Were friendship quilts called album quilts? Did they differ?

54. Was there any significance to the Double Wedding Ring pattern?

55. Were fancier quilts reserved for special gifts?
   What about the bride's quilt?
   Were certain patterns reserved for the bride's quilt (Rose of Sharon)?
   Was a bride allowed to snap her own quilt? Allowed to quilt it?

56. Did you ever sign or date a quilt?
   When and for whom?
   Repeatedly or infrequently?
   Were many quilts signed or dated?

57. Ever hear of a mourning quilt?
   A legacy quilt reflecting the different stages in someone's life?
   Ever hear of a string quilt?
   Were quilts ever done as copies of a favorite old quilt?
   Examples:

58. How many quilts were used on each bed? Winter as contrasted to summer?
   In combination with what other bedding?
   Were beds ever made without quilts?

59. How were quilts and comforts cleaned? How often?
   Did you hang out quilts rather than wash them?
   Did this vary?

60. What was the size of most quilts?
   How far down were they supposed to hang on a bed?
   Were dust ruffles ever used?
   Were quilts tucked in or draped over the bed?
   Did you make quilts of other sizes: crib, trundle, or doll?

61. Did most or all women quilt?
   Did this begin to change? Why?
   When was the golden age of quilting in your community?
   On what did you base your judgment of above question—number of quilters? Quality of design? Quality of needlework?
   When was the low point?
   How do you feel it compares today? What is its future?
   Was quilting ever out of fashion? Were ever people not quilting?

62. Did men or young boys ever quilt or do the piece work?
   Did they have any voice in quiltmaking? In making a design?

63. Where did you get your first frame?
   What type was it?
   Did you ever get another?
   Where did others who quilted get theirs?
   Which type did you prefer? Why?
   What did frames cost?
   How was it determined who sat around a frame and where?
   Were left-handed quilters put in any particular place at the frame?

64. Where did one get quilt clamps?
   Did you ever use a sewing bird?

65. In what room of your home did you quilt?
   Any particular time of the day or year more than another?
   Was the frame up periodically, constantly, or constantly within a season?
   Did you ever quilt out-of-doors?

66. Did you look forward to quilting?
   Would you rather quilt than _____?
   Did you ever try to get out of a quilting assignment?

67. How many years did you make quilts?
   Did you ever stop and why?
   How much a part of your life was quilting: small, moderately important, or very?
   In the lives of your friends or relatives?
   Was your family supportive of your quilting interests?

68. Rate the following functions of a quilt from 1 (as low) to 10 (as high):
   as an expression of love
   as a creative outlet in color and design
   to fill utilitarian needs and considerations (warmth and protection)
   as a link of past to present (continuity of tradition)
   as a display of womanly virtues and a showplace for skills
   as a time for reflection and relaxation
   as a chore which brought one together with a friend or friends
   as an occasion to go out and to break up periods of isolation
   as revenue producing
   as therapy in getting past problems and occupying one's time
   as a romantic attachment to earlier, simpler, better times?

69. Did you strive for perfection in your quilts?
   Did you ever hear that something might be left imperfect since "only God makes something perfect"?
   Did you ever hear any other expressions about quiltmaking such as, "Don't make the stitches too big or you'll catch your toenails."

70. Do you consider quiltmaking an art form? Explain.

71. Can you suggest others that we should contact regarding this project?

Bibliography

Albacete, M. J., and Sharon D'Atri and Jane Reeves. *Ohio Quilts/A Living Tradition.* Canton, Ohio: The Canton Art Institute, 1981.

Album of Favorite Quilting Designs. Pittsburgh: Pennsylvania Farmer, n. d.

The American Agriculturalist, 1800-1905.

Arthur's Home Magazine or *The American Home Magazine,* 1852-1898.

Bacon, Lenice Ingram. *American Patchwork Quilts.* New York: William Morrow & Co., Inc., 1973.

Bank, Mirra. *Anonymous Was a Woman.* New York: St. Martins Press, 1979.

Betterton, Sheila. *The American Quilt Tradition.* The American Museum in Britain, 1976.

Beyer, Jinny. *The Quilters Album of Blocks and Borders.* McLean, Virginia: EPM Publications, 1980.

Binney, Edward, III and Gail Binney-Winslow. *Homage to Amanda/Two Hundred Years of American Quilts.* San Francisco: RK Press, 1984.

Bishop, Robert and Elizabeth Safanda. *A Gallery of Amish Quilts: Design Diversity From a Plain People.* New York: Dutton, 1976.

Bishop, Robert and Patricia Colbentz. *New Discoveries in American Quilts.* New York: Dutton, 1975.

Bowen, Helen. "The Ancient Art of Quilting" *Antiques,* 3: 113-117, March 1923.

_____ . "Corded and Padded Quilting" *Antiques,* 6: 250-253, November 1924.

Burnham, Dorothy K. *Pieced Quilts of Ontario.* Toronto: Royal Ontario Museum, 1975.

Carlisle, Lillian Baker. *Pieced Work and Applique Quilts at Shelburne Museum.* Shelburne, Vermont: Shelburne Museum, 1957.

Catalog of Patchwork Quilts. Chicago, Illinois: Needlecraft Supply Co., 1939.

Caulfield, S. F. A. and Blanche C. Saward. *The Dictionary of Needlework, An Encyclopedia of Artistic, Plain and Fancy Needlework.* London: L. Upcott Gill, 1882.

Child, Lydia Maria. *The Girls Own Book.* New York: Clark Austin, 1833.

Clabburn, Pamela. *Patchwork.* Aylesbury, England: Shire Publications, 1983.

Clark, Mary Washington. *Kentucky Quilts and Their Makers.* Lexington: University Press of Kentucky, 1976.

Clark, Rickey. *Quilts and Carousels: Folk Art in the Firelands.* Oberlin, Ohio: Firelands Association for the Visual Arts, 1983.

Colby, Averil. *Patchwork.* London: B. T. Batsford. Ltd., 1958.

_____ . *Quilting.* New York: Charles Scribner's Sons, 1971.

Cooper, Patricia and Norma Bradley Buferd. *The Quilters. Women And Domestic Art.* Garden City, New York: Doubleday & Company, Inc., 1977.

Curtis, Phillip. *American Quilts.* Newark, New Jersey: Newark Museum, 1973.

Davidson, Mildred. *American Quilts From the Art Institute of Chicago.* Chicago: The Art Institute of Chicago, 1966.

The Delineator or *The Designer and The Woman's Magazine.* 1895-1926.

Demorest's Family Magazine. 1886-1888.

Directory of Prominent Business Places in Lewisburg, PA. Lewisburg: Shamp & Askins, 1880.

Dyer, Margie. *Pennsylvania German Quilts.* New York: Goethe House, 1983.

Earle, Alice Morse. *Home Life in Colonial Days.* New York: Macmillan Company, 1898.

Eaton, Allen H. *Handicrafts of the Southern Highlands.* New York: Russell Sage Foundation, 1937.

Echelman, E. M. "Juscht En Deppich," *The Pennsylvania German.* Vol. VII, No. 5, September, 1906, pp. 203-204.

Estate inventories and vendues. Union and Snyder counties, Pennsylvania. 1839-1855; for Union County 1856-1880.

Finley, Ruth E. *Old Patchwork Quilts and the Women Who Made Them.* Philadelphia: J. B. Lippincott & Co., 1929.

Fisher, H. L. *Olden Times: or Pennsylvania Rural Life Some Fifty Years Ago.* York: Fisher Brothers, 1888.

Fitzrandolph, Mavis. *Traditional Quilting. Its Story and Practice.* London: B. T. Batsford, 1954.

Fox, Sandi. *19th Century American Patchwork Quilt.* Tokyo, Japan: The Seibu Museum of Art, 1983.

_____ . *Quilts in Utah/A Reflection of the Western Experience.* n.p., n.d.

Frost, S. Annie. *The Ladies Guide to Needlework, Embroideries, Etc.* 1877.

Fry, Thomas L. *American Quilts/A Handmade Legacy.* Oakland, California: The Oakland Museum, 1981.

Garrad, Larch S. "Quilting and Patchwork in the Isle of Man," *A Journal of Ethnological Studies/Folk Life,* 1979, pp. 39-48.

Garvan, Beatrice B. and Charles F. Hummel. *The Pennsylvania Germans/A Celebrations of Their Arts 1683-1853.* Philadelphia: Philadelphia Museum of Arts; 1983.

Gibbons, Phebe Earle. *Pennsylvania Dutch and Other Essays.* Philadelphia: J. B. Lippincott & Co., 1882.

Godey's Lady's Book. 1830-1897.

Good Housekeeping. 1885-1940.

Graeff, Marie Knorr. *Pennsylvania German Quilts.* Home Craft Course, Vol. XIV., 1964.

Grandmother Clark's & Authentic Early American Patchwork Quilts. St. Louis, Missouri: W. L. M. Clark, 1932.

Grit, Williamsport. 1882-1924.

Haders, Phyllis. *Sunshine and Shadow. The Amish and Their Quilts.* New York: Universe Books/The Main Street Press, 1976.

Hale, Sarah. *Mrs. Hale's Receipts for the Million.* Philadelphia: Peterson, 1857.

Hall, Carrie A. and Rose G. Kretsinger. *The Romance of the Patchwork Quilt in America.* Caldwell, Idaho: Caxton Printers Ltd., Bonanza Books, 1935.

Holstein, Jonathan. *Abstract Design in American Quilts.* New York: Whitney Museum of Art, 1971.

_____ . *Kentucky Quilts 1800-1900/The Kentucky Quilt Project.* New York: Pantheon Books, 1982.

_____ . *The Pieced Quilt/An American Design Tradition.* Boston: New York Graphic Society; Little, Brown and Company, 1973.

House Beautiful. 1897-1930.

Ickis, Marguerite. *The Standard Book of Quilt Making and Collecting.* New York: Dover Publications Inc., 1959 (rpt.) 1949.

Instructions For Patchwork. n.p.: J. F. Ingalls, 1884.

Jeffery, G.G. *Rugs & Quilts,* London: Oxford University Press, 1943.

Katzenburg, Dena S. *Baltimore Album Quilts.* Baltimore: The Baltimore Museum of Art, 1980.

_____ . *The Great American Cover-Up/Counterpanes of the Eighteenth and Nineteenth Centuries.* Baltimore: The Baltimore Museum of Art, 1971.

Keyser, Alan G. "Beds, Bedding, Bedsteads and Sleep," *The Quarterly of Pennsylvania German Society,* The Pennsylvania German Society: Breinigsville, Pennsylvania, October, 1978, pp. 1-28.

King, Elizabeth. *Quilting.* New York: Leisure League of America, 1934.

Kiracofe, Roderick and Michael Kile. *The Quilt Digest.* San Francisco: Kirakofe and Kile, 1983-1985.

Ladies' Art Company Catalogs. St. Louis, Missouri: Ladies' Art Company, 1898-1928.

Ladies Home Journal. 1892-1907.

Ladies Manual of Fancy Work. Vol. 3 No. 3, April 1903.

Ladies Magazine. 1834-1836.

Ladies National Magazine. 1844-1845, 1880-1881.

Ladies Register and Housewife's Almanack. 1844.

Leslie, Eliza. *American Girl's Book* or *Occupation for Play Hours.* New York: R. Worthington, 16th ed. 1879.

_____ . *The House Book.* Philadelphia: Cary & Hart, 1840.

MacDowell, Marsha. "Michigan Quilts" *Michigan History,* July-August 1984, pp. 32-34.

McKim, Ruby. *One Hundred and One Patchwork Patterns.* Independence, Missouri: McKim Studios, 1931.

McElwain, Mary A. *Notes on Applied Work and Patchwork.* London: His Majesty's Stationery Office, 1949.

_____ . *Notes on Quilting.* London: His Majesty's Stationery Office, 1949.

_____. *The Romance of Village Quilts*. Walworth, Wisconsin: n.p., 1936.

McMorris, Penny. *Crazy Quilts*. New York: E. P. Dutton, 1984.

Montgomery, Florence. *Printed Textiles/English and American Cottons and Linens*. New York: The Viking Press, 1970.

Mountain Artisans. Providence, Rhode Island: Rhode Island School of Design, 1970.

Mountain Mist quilt wrappers, 1931-1939.

The Mountain Mist Blue Book of Quilts. Cincinnati, Ohio: Stearns and Foster Company, 1937.

The National Stockman and Farmer or *The Pennsylvania Stockman and Farmer*, 1884-1928.

Needlecraft. 1900-1928.

New Jersey Quilters/A Timeless Tradition. Morristown, New Jersey: Morristown Museum of Arts and Sciences, 1982.

North Carolina Country Quilts. Chapel Hill, North Carolina: The Ackland Art Museum, 1978.

Orlofsky, Patsy and Myron. *Quilts in America*. New York: McGraw-Hill Book Company, 1974.

Pennsylvania Quilts, *One Hundred Years, 1830-1930*. Philadelphia: Moore College of Art, 1978.

Peterson, Harold. *American Interiors from Colonial Times to the Late Victorians*. New York: Charles Scribner's Sons, 1971.

Peterson's Magazine. 1843-1891.

Peto, Florence, *American Quilts and Coverlets/A History of a Charming Native Art Together With a Manual of Instruction for Beginners*. New York: Chanticleer Press, 1949.

_____. *Historic Quilts*. New York: American Historical Company, 1939.

Pettit, Florence H. *America's Printed and Painted Fabrics 1600-1900*. New York: Hastings House, 1970.

Pottinger, David. *Quilts From the Indiana Amish/A Regional Collection*. New York: E. P. Dutton, 1983.

Pullan, Mrs. *Ladies Manual of Fancy Work*. New York: Dick Fitzgerald, Publishers, 1859.

Quilters Newsletter, 1972-1984.

Roan, Nancy and Ellen J. Gehret. *Just a Quilt or Juscht en Deppich*. Green Lane, Pennsylvania: Goschenhoppen Historians, 1984.

Robacker, Earl F. *Old Stuff in Up-Country Pennsylvania*. New York: A. S. Barnes and Company, 1973.

Robertson, Elizabeth Wells. *American Quilts*. New York: Studio Publications, Inc., 1948.

Safford, Carleton L. and Bishop, Robert. *American Quilts and Coverlets*. New York: E. P. Dutton & Company, Inc., 1972.

Sater, Joel. *The Patchwork Quilt*. Ephrata, Pennsylvania: Science Press, 1981.

Schiffer, Margaret B. *Chester County, Pennsylvania Inventories, 1684-1850*. Exton, Pennsylvania: Schiffer Publishing, Ltd., 1974.

Sears Century of Progress in Quiltmaking. Chicago: Sears, Roebuck & Co., 1934.

Sexton, Carlie. *Early American Quilts*. Southampton, New York: Crackerbarrel Press, 1924.

_____. *Yesterdays Quilts in Homes of Today*. Des Moines, Iowa: Meredith Publishing Company, 1930.

Snow, Virginia. *Quilting Designs*. Elgin, Illinois: Virginia Snow Studios, n.d.

Swan, Susan Burrows. "Household Textiles" *The Art of the Pennsylvania Germans*. New York: W. W. Norton & Co., 1983.

Uncoverings. Mill Valley, California: The American Quilt Study Group, 1981-1985.

Union County newspapers. 1833-1891.

The Universal Entertainer. 1743-1753.

Ward, Anne. "Quilting in the North of England," *A Journal of the Society for Folk Life Studies*, 1966, pp. 75-81.

Webster, Marie D. *Quilts: Their Story and How to Make Them*. New York: Doubleday, Page and Company, 1915.

White, Margaret E. *Quilts and Counterpanes in the Newark Museum*. Newark, New Jersey: The Newark Museum, 1948.

Woodward, Thomas K. and Blanche Greenstein. *Crib Quilts and Other Small Wonders*. New York: E. P. Dutton, 1981.

Quilters Choice. Lawrence, Kansas: Helen Foresman Spenser Museum of Art, 1978.

Quilts and Coverlets. Denver, Colorado: The Denver Art Museum, 1974.

Documentation Day Informants

New Berlin: Erma Boyer, Mifflinburg; Kathy Brouse, Middleburg; Ethel Herman, New Berlin; Blanche Kulp, Snydertown; Beatrice Miller, Mifflinburg; Mary Moll and Jeanne Sauers, New Berlin; Margaret and Miriam Seebold, Mifflinburg; Margaret Solomon, New Berlin; Ardie Strauser, Northumberland; Lillian Tresca, Snydertown; Pauline Wehr, Mifflinburg; Marie Wolfe, New Berlin; Ruth Wehr Zimmerman, Mifflinburg.

Laurelton: Harry Bingaman, Laurelton; Priscilla Chick and Rosalie Engelhardt, Millmont; Dorothy Knauss, Mifflinburg; Miriam Kreisher, Laurelton; Virginia Martin, Margaret Moyer and Donna Pervis, Millmont; Dorothy Reiner, Swengel; Virginia Schneeberg and Doris Scott, Laurelton.

Lewisburg: Mrs. Fred Brouse, Evelyn J. Frantz and Nada Gray, Lewisburg; Mary Maher, Sara Heiser Reigel and Cherry Will, Buffalo Crossroads; Lee Saxton, Millmont; Janice Snyder and Elmer Stahl, Mazeppa; Slifer House Museum, Lewisburg; Harold Walters, Lewisburg; Heather Renne Wolf, Turbotville.

Mifflinburg: Mary Arnold, Charles Beaver, Mrs. William Conrad, Jr., Linda Boyer and Linda Campbell, Mifflinburg; Gladys Coleman, Caroline and Robert Criswell, Anna Dieffenderfer, Lewisburg; Mrs. Richard Erdley, Mifflinburg; Mrs. Richard Facer, Winfield; Joseph Foster, Mifflinburg; Ann Gelnett, Lewisburg; Mrs. William Harter, Mifflinburg; Frances Hartley, Middleburg; Jack Hursh, Mrs. Donald Hoy, Mary Iddings, Mrs. Harry Keefer, Marguerite Kieffer, Helen Kerstetter, and Mary Koons, Mifflinburg; Diana and Jeannette Lasansky, Lewisburg; Lou Jane Mitchell, Mifflinburg; Sonja Noll, New Columbia; Pauline Poggi, Miriam Prutzman, Beatrice Reed, Pauline Rotering, Katherine Roush, and Dorothy Ruhl, Mifflinburg; Ethel and George Ruhl and Edna Sheary, Lewisburg; Laura Shirk, Mifflinburg; Beulah and Gary Slear, Lewisburg; Nancy Snook, Catherine Snyder, Olive Stamm, Mifflinburg; Union County Historical Society; Gwen Watson and Pauline Wehr, Mifflinburg.

New Columbia: Pearl Platt Coup, New Columbia; Katherine Hackenberg, New Berlin; Mrs. Leroy Kling, West Milton; Nancy Coup, New Columbia; Jane Watson, Mifflinburg; Allen and Anna Wehr, Mifflinburg; J. S. Ziegler, Lewisburg.

Sunbury and Shamokin: Verna Bahner Bzdil. Sunbury; Madeline Drinkhouse, Shamokin; Mary Fegger, Sunbury; Diane Garcia, Shamokin; Mary Haas, Winfield; Mary Hile, Shamokin; Arlene Kerstetter, Sunbury; Bertha Lees, Allentown; Nancy Bahner Neff, Sunbury; Helen Pfleegor, Milton; Rachael Reed, State College; Elva Sacona, Shamokin; Catherine Stahl, Northumberland; Trinity Lutheran Church, Shamokin; Mrs. Fred Troxell and Pauline Udebye, Northumberland; Leona Wirt, Helen Wolfe, and Mark Wynn, Sunbury.

Williamsport: Reba Bastian and Harold Biehler, Williamsport; Mrs. William Bierly, Jersey Shore; Georgia Burch, Williamsport; Gertrude Bitner, Jersey Shore; Rev. and Mrs. Raymond Byler, Williamsport; Bess Clarke, Canton; Christine Cocks and Mrs. Kenneth Cooper, Williamsport; Beth Confer, Cogan Station; Kathryn Deebel and Mrs. Richard Dingle, Williamsport; Kim Fisher, Jersey Shore; David Fulmer, Williamsport; Mrs. Elvin Fry, Allenwood; Mary Girton, Williamsport; Esther Hastings, Avis; Marian Hess, Marguerite Hill, William Hopler, Jane Dawn Keiper, and Lycoming County Historical Society, Williamsport; Margaret Mark, South Williamsport; Helen McCourt, Wilhelmena Mikusinski, and Dolores Miller, Williamsport; Mrs. R. S. Pepperman, Linden; Debi Porter, Kathy Radspinner, Thelma Raymond and Helen Rick, Williamsport; Louise Reish, Centre Hall; Margaret Schmelzle, Mrs. Harold Shultz, Mary Smith, and Mrs. Arch Troxell, Williamsport; Mrs. Herbert Walker, Avis; Catheal Weiser, Montoursville; Mrs. John Winter, Rev. Melvin Witmire, and Mrs. Richard Wittig, Williamsport; Mrs. Russell Woolever, Jr., South Williamsport; Charles and Mildred Young, Williamsport.

Aaronsburg: Lorraine Cato, New Hampshire; Goldie Copenhauer, Sara Fiedler, Tammie Gramley, Iva Hosterman, Marion Long, Patti McDonald, and Gladys Stover, Aaronsburg.

Lock Haven: Dorothy Bailey, Tamarack; Betty Baird, Lock Haven; Mrs. Stanley Barker, North Bend; Betty Bryertown, Lock Haven; Charlotte Crider, Renovo; Clinton County Historical Society and Jeanne Collins Dickey, Lock Haven; Genevieve Earon, Flemington; Mildred Fox and Lydia Furst, Mackeyville; Nancy Gilbert, Jersey Shore; Dr. Carl Guerriere, Boiling Springs; Joyce Gummo, Beech Creek; Susan Hannegan, Mill Hall; Mrs. S. B. Hardy, Flemington; Laura Heggenstaller, Loganton; Elizabeth Jeselnick, Renovo; Arlene Keller, Mill Hall; Carole Kidder, Lock Haven; Patricia Kline, Waterville; Dorothy Klinefelter, Loganton; Barbara Kulak, Lock Haven; Kathryn Kyle, Mackeyville; Barbara Long, Lock Haven; Edward Long, Flemington; Nellie Lucas, Beech Creek; Helen Markle, Lock Haven; Christina and John Martin, Howard; Carolina McConaghay and Evelyn McKeague, Renovo; Lois Miller, Salona; Margaret Munro, Lock Haven; Marian Nihardt, Mill Hall; Isabell Packer, Mackeyville; Mrs. G. Wesley Pedlow, Jr., Lock Haven; Edith Romig, Lamar; Mary Jane Sarvey, Lock Haven; Emogene Smeltzer, Mill Hall; Earl Streck, Beech Creek; Ruth Smith, Mill Hall; Margaret Thomas, Blanchard; Vera Voneda, Mackeyville; Betty Wallinger, Lock Haven; Vivian Welsh, Mill Hall; Dora Wenker, Lock Haven; Mrs. Allan Williams, Weatherly; Peggy Wilson, Lock Haven; Ethel Yearick, Mill Hall; Jeannette Zimmerman, Lock Haven.

Bellefonte: Wilma Aumiller, Bellefonte; Jane Barber, State College, Mrs. Joseph Blair, Williamsport; Mrs. Paul Breon, Centre Hall; Gloria Braun, Boalsburg; Centre County Historical Museum and Library and Paul Corman, Bellefonte; Vivian Hench, State College; Irene Kellerman, Milesburg; Mrs. Paul Kendig, State College; Kay Koon, Port Matilda; James Kustenbauter, Bellefonte; Marguerite Lingle, State College; Ralph Long, Centre Hall; Helen Love, State College; Jessie Lykens, Port Matilda; Louise May, Bessie Mensch, and Helen Murdock, Bellefonte; Rose Park, State College; Carolyn Petrus, State College; Louise Reisch, Centre Hall; Frances Ridge, Bellefonte; Alma Shope, State College; Jean Smith, Virginia Ulrich and Mrs. Harter Vonada, Bellefonte.

Lewistown: Frances Barnes, Belleville; Martha Barnes, Lewistown; Helen Bratton, McVeytown; Edna Chester, Belleville; Mary Anna Cressman, T. R. Culbertson and Dorothy Dunion, Lewistown; Elizabeth Fortmann, State College; Margaret Harpster, Burnham; Marion Johns, Robert Karn, Lois Kling, Laura Latcha, Thekla Leeper, and Helen McMullen, Lewistown; Pauline McNabb, Burnham; Mifflin County Historical Society and Pauline Miller, Lewistown; Mary Reed, Reedsville; Eva Rearick, Milroy; Leah Rearick, Riversburgh; Eloise Reigle, Reedsville; Mrs. Hershel Rittenhouse, Josephine Shellenberg, Ruth Snyder, and Audrey Treaster, Lewistown; Sarah Ward, Belleville; Harry and Thelma Yocum, Lewistown.

Other: Helen Aucker, Port Trevorton; Irene Bingaman, Laurelton; Jim and Carol Bohn, Mifflinburg; Cora Boop, Laurelton; Dona Crone, Elysburg; Maude Engel, Lewisburg; Eve Granick and David Wheatcroft, Lewisburg; Ada Herman, New Berlin; Laura Keiser, Lewisburg; Shirley and Robert Kuster, Selinsgrove; Hilda Jeffries, Carroll; Evelyn Mabus, Amos and John Persing, Lewisburg; Bessie Shiffer, New Berlin; Florence Shively, Millmont; Mrs. Ray Shively, Laurelton; Robert Shoemaker, Vicksburg; Sara Hoffman Sinot, Millmont; Blanche Snyder, Lewisburg; Tama Thompson, Loganton; Irving and Ellie Williams, Lewisburg; Nora and Mrs. Roy Zimmerman, Hartleton.

Correspondence

Barbara Brackman, Lawrence, Kansas; Elizabeth Grimm, Missouri; Historical Society, St. Louis, Missouri; David Leiby, Cincinnati, Ohio; Leonare Swoiskin, Sears Roebuck, and Co., Chicago; John Vidosh, Sunbury; Edith Welsh, Lancaster.

Index